"John MacArthur expertly and lucidly explains that Jesus frees us from bondage into a royal slavery that we might be His possession. Those who would be His children must, paradoxically, be willing to be His slaves."

—DR. R. C. SPROUL

"So much of our Christian walk is focused on 'self'—how will this trial refine my faith, improve my character, or fit into a pattern for my good? Often when believers speak of a personal Savior, they mean a Savior who is personally committed to their health, success, and life fulfillment. But such a view couldn't be farther from the truth. In his new book, John MacArthur presents a powerfully riveting and truly eye-opening look at our relationship to the Lord Jesus. Want to rise to a new level of trust and confidence in your Master? Then this is the book for you!"

—JONI EARECKSON TADA, JONI AND FRIENDS
INTERNATIONAL DISABILITY CENTER

"Dr. John MacArthur is never afraid to tell the truth and in this book he does just that. The Christian's great privilege is to be the slave of Christ. Dr. MacArthur makes it clear that this is one of the Bible's most succinct ways of describing our discipleship. This is a powerful exposition of Scripture, a convincing, corrective to shallow Christianity, a masterful work of pastoral encouragement . . . a devotional classic."

—DR. R. ALBERT MOHLER
PRESIDENT, THE SOUTHERN BAPTIST THEOLOGICAL SEMINARY

"Dr. John MacArthur's teaching on 'slavery' resonates in the deepest recesses of my 'inner-man.' As an African-American pastor, I have been there. That is why the thought of someone writing about slavery as being a 'God-send' was the most ludicrous, unconscionable thing that I could have ever imagined . . . until I read this book. Now I see that becoming a slave is a biblical command, completely redefining the idea of freedom in Christ. I don't want to simply be a 'follower' or even just a 'servant' . . . but a 'slave.'"

—THE REV. DR. DALLAS H. WILSON JR.
VICAR, ST. JOHN'S EPISCOPAL CHAPEL
CHARLESTON, SOUTH CAROLINA

slave

slave

The Hidden Truth about Your Identity in Christ

JOHN MACARTHUR

THOMAS NELSON
Since 1798

NASHVILLE   DALLAS   MEXICO CITY   RIO DE JANEIRO

Slave

© 2010 by John MacArthur

Published in Nashville, Tennessee, by Thomas Nelson. Thomas Nelson is a trademark of Thomas Nelson, Inc.

Published in association with the literary agency of Wolgemuth & Associates, Inc.

Unless otherwise noted, Scripture quotations are taken from the New American Standard Bible.® © The Lockman Foundation 1960, 1962, 1963, 1968, 1971, 1972, 1973, 1975, 1977, 1995. Used by permission.

Scriptures marked NKJV are taken from the New King James Version. © 1982 by Thomas Nelson, Inc. Used by permission. All rights reserved.

Scriptures marked HCSB are taken from the Holman Christian Standard Bible.© 1999, 2000, 2002, 2003 by Broadman and Holman Publishers. All rights reserved.

Thomas Nelson, Inc., titles may be purchased in bulk for educational, business, fund-raising, or sales promotional use. For information, please e-mail SpecialMarkets@ThomasNelson.com.

ISBN: 978-1-4002-8111-4 (IE)

Library of Congress Cataloging-in-Publication Data

MacArthur, John, 1939–
  Slave : the hidden truth about your identity in Christ / John MacArthur.
    p. cm.
  ISBN 978-1-4002-0207-2
  1. Identification (Religion) 2. Christian life. I. Title. II. Title: Hidden truth about your identity in Christ.
  BV4509.5.M2525 2011
  248.4—dc22   2010032926

Printed in the United States of America

10 11 12 13 14 15 QG 10 9 8 7 6 5 4 3 2 1

Contents

To Nathan Busenitz

Wise and accomplished beyond his years, he has proven to be a treasure to me in multiple ways. He has served me as a personal assistant in pastoral ministry, as a writer of many articles on the Pulpit blog, as a fellow elder teaching and preaching at Grace Community Church, and as a professor at The Master's Seminary. He has applied both his mind and heart to the research and writing of this book. He is as committed to its truth and urgency as I am. The dedication can only be to him so that all who read it in the years to come will know of my gratitude for his efforts.

Preface

After more than fifty years of translating, studying, teaching, preaching, and writing through the New Testament, I thought I had its truths pretty well identified and understood—especially in the realm of the New Testament theology of the gospel. In fact, clarifying the gospel was the most important and constant emphasis of my writing—from *The Gospel According to Jesus*, *Ashamed of the Gospel*, *Hard to Believe*, and *The Truth War* to countless sermons and articles through the years. But through all those efforts, a profound and comprehensive perspective, one that dominates the New Testament and is crucial to the gospel, escaped me and almost everyone else.

It wasn't until the spring of 2007, on an all-night flight to London while reading *Slave of Christ* by Murray J. Harris, that I realized there had been a centuries-long cover-up by English New Testament translators that had obscured a precious, powerful, and clarifying revelation by the Holy Spirit. Undoubtedly, the cover-up was not intentional—at least not initially. Yet its results have been dramatically serious.

A cover-up in the English New Testament translations? Was that true? Why? And with what consequences? Had no one uncovered this before Harris in 1999?

It didn't take long to find one who had—Edwin Yamauchi in his 1966 *Bulletin of the Evangelical Theological Society* article entitled "Slaves of God." Why had there been no response to his work? And how could a truth related so essentially not only to translation integrity but also to New Testament teaching about our relation to Christ be purposely hidden and the cover-up ignored?

I also discovered in my trips around the world that there are many other major language translators who have followed the lead of the English versions and maintained the cover-up. Yet there are some who do translate the word correctly. Thus this revelation is not hidden to my fellow believers in places like Russia, Romania, Indonesia, and the Philippines. Why in English?

I have no doubt that this perpetual hiding of an essential element of New Testament revelation has contributed to much of the confusion in evangelical teaching and practice. In fact, I wonder if it wasn't the reason I felt the need to write so many books to clarify the gospel. If this one reality had been known, would any of those books have been necessary?

As I began to dig down into this buried jewel of the gospel, its pervasive splendor began to dominate my thinking and preaching. Every time and everywhere I addressed the subject, the response was the same—startled wonder.

During the same period I was asked to write a book on the "doctrines of grace" that was faithful to the Reformers. Was another one really necessary? Who could improve on Calvin, Luther, the English Puritans, Edwards, or Spurgeon? Certainly not me. I couldn't hope to add to the clear, complete, and enduring works of past and present theologians on gospel themes. So I struggled to find a reason to write something new, considering what had already been written.

Until I saw the cover-up.

Though all those noble theologians in the rich Reformation tradition of gospel truth touched on this matter—no one had pulled the hidden jewel all the way into the sunlight.

Thus this book. As you read it, my prayer is that you will see the riches of your salvation in a radically new way.

—John MacArthur

one

One Hidden Word

I am a Christian."

The young man said nothing else as he stood before the Roman governor, his life hanging in the balance. His accusers pressed him again, hoping to trip him up or force him to recant. But once more he answered with the same short phrase. "I am a Christian."

It was the middle of the second century, during the reign of emperor Marcus Aurelius.[1] Christianity was illegal, and believers throughout the Roman Empire faced the threat of imprisonment, torture, or death. Persecution was especially intense in southern Europe, where Sanctus, a deacon from Vienna, had been arrested and brought to trial. The young man was repeatedly told to renounce the faith he professed. But his resolve was undeterred. "I am a Christian."

No matter what question he was asked, he always gave the same unchanging answer. According to the ancient church historian Eusebius, Sanctus "girded himself against [his accusers] with such firmness that he would not even tell his name, or the nation or city to which he belonged, or whether he was bond or free, but answered in the

_____

1. Marcus Aurelius reigned from AD 161 to 180. The intense persecution described here likely took place around 177.

Roman tongue to all their questions, 'I am a Christian.'"[2] When at last it became obvious that he would say nothing else, he was condemned to severe torture and a public death in the amphitheater. On the day of his execution, he was forced to run the gauntlet, subjected to wild beasts, and fastened to a chair of burning iron. Throughout all of it, his accusers kept trying to break him, convinced that his resistance would crack under the pain of torment. But as Eusebius recounted, "Even thus they did not hear a word from Sanctus except the confession which he had uttered from the beginning."[3] His dying words told of an undying commitment. His rallying cry remained constant throughout his entire trial. "I am a Christian."

For Sanctus, his whole identity—including his name, citizenship, and social status—was found in Jesus Christ. Hence, no better answer could have been given to the questions he was asked. He was a *Christian*, and that designation defined everything about him.

This same perspective was shared by countless others in the early church. It fueled their witness, strengthened their resolve, and confounded their opponents. When arrested, these courageous believers would confidently respond as Sanctus had, with a succinct assertion of their loyalty to Christ. As one historian explained about the early martyrs,

> They [would reply] to all questionings about them [with] the short
> but comprehensive answer, "I am a Christian." Again and again they
> caused no little perplexity to their judges by the pertinacity with

2. Eusebius, *Church History*, 5.1.20, quoted in Philip Schaff, *Nicene and Post-Nicene Fathers*, 2nd ser. (Grand Rapids: Eerdmans, 1971), I:214. (Hereafter, *Nicene and Post-Nicene Fathers* will be referred to as *NPNF*.)

3. Ibid.

which they adhered to this brief profession of faith. The question was repeated, "Who are you?" and they replied, "I have already said that I am a Christian; and he who says that has thereby named his country, his family, his profession, and all things else besides."[4]

Following Jesus Christ was the sum of their entire existence.[5] At the moment when life itself was on the line, nothing else mattered besides identifying themselves with Him.

For these faithful believers, the name "Christian" was much more than just a general religious designation. It defined everything about them, including how they viewed both themselves and the world around them. The label underscored their love for a crucified Messiah along with their willingness to follow Him no matter the cost. It told of the wholesale transformation God had produced in their hearts, and witnessed to the fact that they had been made completely new in Him. They had died to their old way of life, having been born again into the family of God. *Christian* was not simply a title, but an entirely new way of thinking—one that had serious implications for how they lived—and ultimately how they died.

---

4. J. Spencer Northcote, *Epitaphs of the Catacombs or Christian Inscriptions in Rome during the First Four Centuries* (London: Longman, Green & Co., 1878; repr., Whitefish, MT: Kessinger Publishing, 2007), 139.

5. Such was the attitude of Ignatius, a pastor from Antioch and a disciple of the apostle John. Upon being condemned to death in Rome (around AD 110), Ignatius wrote, "It is not that I want merely to be called a Christian, but actually to be one. Yes, if I prove to be one [by being faithful to the end], then I can have the name. . . . Come fire, cross, battling with wild beasts, wrenching of bones, mangling of limbs, crushing of my whole body, cruel tortures of the devil—only let me get to Jesus Christ!" (Ignatius, *Epistle to the Romans*, 3, 5, 6, quoted in Cyril C. Richardson, *Early Church Fathers* [Louisville, KY: Westminster John Knox Press, 1953], 104–5).

What Does It Mean to Be a Christian?

The early martyrs were crystal clear on what it meant to be a Christian. But ask what it means today and you're likely to get a wide variety of answers, even from those who identify themselves with the label.

For some, being "Christian" is primarily cultural and traditional, a nominal title inherited from a previous generation, the net effect of which involves avoiding certain behaviors and occasionally attending church. For others, being a Christian is largely political, a quest to defend moral values in the public square or perhaps to preserve those values by withdrawing from the public square altogether. Still more define Christianity in terms of a past religious experience, a general belief in Jesus, or a desire to be a good person. Yet all of these fall woefully short of what it truly means to be a Christian from a biblical perspective.

Interestingly, the followers of Jesus Christ were not called "Christians" until ten to fifteen years after the church began. Before that time, they were known simply as disciples, brothers, believers, saints, and followers of the Way (a title derived from Christ's reference to Himself, in John 14:6, as "the way, the truth, and the life" [NKJV]). According to Acts 11:26, it was in Antioch of Syria that "the disciples were first called Christians" and since that time the label has stuck.

The name was initially coined by unbelievers as an attempt to deride those who followed a crucified Christ.[6] But what began as a ridicule soon became a badge of honor. To be called "Christians" (in Greek, *Christianoi*) was to be identified as Jesus' disciples and to be associated with Him as loyal followers. In a similar fashion, those in Caesar's

---

6. As the apostle Paul explains in 1 Corinthians 1:23, the idea of a crucified Christ was "to the Jews a stumbling block and to the Greeks foolishness" (NKJV). Those who followed Jesus Christ (having been labeled as Christians) were denounced as heretics by unbelieving Jews and derided as fools by unbelieving Gentiles.

household would refer to themselves as *Kaisarianoi* ("those of Caesar") in order to show their deep allegiance to the Roman Emperor. Unlike the *Kaisarianoi*, however, the Christians did not give their ultimate allegiance to Rome or any other earthly power; their full dedication and worship were reserved for Jesus Christ alone.

Thus, to be a *Christian*, in the true sense of the term, is to be a wholehearted follower of Jesus Christ. As the Lord Himself said in John 10:27, "My sheep hear My voice, and I know them, and *they follow Me*" (emphasis added). The name suggests much more than a superficial association with Christ. Rather, it demands a deep affection for Him, allegiance to Him, and submission to His Word. "You are My friends if you do what I command you," Jesus told His disciples in the Upper Room (John 15:14). Earlier He told the crowds who flocked to hear Him, "If you continue in My word, then you are truly disciples of Mine" (John 8:31); and elsewhere: "If anyone wishes to come after Me, he must deny himself, and take up his cross daily and follow Me" (Luke 9:23; cf. John 12:26).

When we call ourselves *Christians*, we proclaim to the world that everything about us, including our very self-identity, is found in Jesus Christ because we have denied our*selves* in order to follow and obey Him. He is both our Savior and our Sovereign, and our lives center on pleasing *Him*. To claim the title is to say with the apostle Paul, "To live is Christ and to die is gain" (Phil. 1:21).

A Word That Changes Everything

Since its first appearance in Antioch, the term *Christian* has become the predominant label for those who follow Jesus. It is an appropriate designation because it rightly focuses on the centerpiece of our faith: Jesus Christ. Yet ironically, the word itself appears only three times in the New Testament—twice in the book of Acts and once in 1 Peter 4:16.

In addition to the name *Christian*, the Bible uses a host of other terms to identify the followers of Jesus. Scripture describes us as aliens and strangers of God, citizens of heaven, and lights to the world. We are heirs of God and joint heirs with Christ, members of His body, sheep in His flock, ambassadors in His service, and friends around His table. We are called to compete like athletes, to fight like soldiers, to abide like branches in a vine, and even to desire His Word as newborn babies long for milk. All of these descriptions—each in its own unique way—help us understand what it means to be a Christian.

Yet, the Bible uses one metaphor more frequently than any of these. It is a word picture you might not expect, but it is absolutely critical for understanding what it means to follow Jesus.

It is the image of a *slave*.

Time and time again throughout the pages of Scripture, believers are referred to as *slaves of God* and *slaves of Christ*.[7] In fact, whereas the outside world called them "Christians," the earliest believers repeatedly referred to themselves in the New Testament as the Lord's slaves.[8] For

---

7. The Hebrew word for slave, *'ebed*, can speak of literal slavery to a human master. But it is also used metaphorically to describe believers (more than 250 times), denoting their duty and privilege to obey the heavenly Lord. The New Testament's use of the Greek word, *doulos*, is similar. It, too, can refer to physical slavery. Yet it is also applied to believers—denoting their relationship to the divine Master—at least 40 times (cf. Murray J. Harris, *Slave of Christ* [Downers Grove, IL: InterVarsity Press, 1999], 20–24). An additional 30-plus NT passages use the language of *doulos* to teach truths about the Christian life.

8. See, for example, Romans 1:1; 1 Corinthians 7:22; Galatians 1:10; Ephesians 6:6; Philippians 1:1; Colossians 4:12; Titus 1:1; James 1:1; 1 Peter 2:16; 2 Peter 1:1; Jude 1; and Revelation 1:1.

them, the two ideas were synonymous. To be a Christian was to be a slave of Christ.[9]

The story of the martyrs confirms that this is precisely what they meant when they declared to their persecutors, "I am a Christian." A young man named Apphianus, for example, was imprisoned and tortured by the Roman authorities. Throughout his trial, he would only reply that he was the slave of Christ.[10] Though he was finally sentenced to death and drowned in the sea, his allegiance to the Lord never wavered.

Other early martyrs responded similarly: "If they consented to amplify their reply, the perplexity of the magistrates was only the more increased, for they seemed to speak insoluble enigmas. 'I am a slave of Caesar,' they said, 'but a Christian who has received his liberty from Christ Himself;' or, contrariwise, 'I am a free man, the slave of Christ;' so that it sometimes happened that it became necessary to send for the proper official (the *curator civitatis*) to ascertain the truth as to their civil condition."[11]

But what proved to be confusing to the Roman authorities made perfect sense to the martyrs of the early church.[12] Their self-identity

9. According to the *International Standard Bible Encyclopedia* (hereinafter referred to as *ISBE*), some commentators have proposed that the term "Christian" literally means "slave of Christ." For example, "Deissmann (*Lict vom Osten*, 286) suggests that *Christian* means *slave of Christ*, as *Caesarian* means *slave of Caesar*" (John Dickie, "Christian," in James Orr, ed., *ISBE* [Chicago: Howard-Severance Company, 1915], I:622).

10. Stringfellow Barr, *The Mask of Jove* (Philadelphia: Lippincott, 1966), 483.

11. Northcote, *Epitaphs of the Catacombs*, 140.

12. Karl Heinrich Rengstorf, under "δοῦλος," in Gerhard Kittel, ed.; Geoffrey Bromiley, trans., *Theological Dictionary of the New Testament*, vol. 2, notes that, "In the early Church the formula [*slave of God* or *slave of Christ*] took on a new lease of life, being used increasingly by Christians in self-designation (cf. 2 Clem. 20, 1; Herm. m. 5, 2, 1; 6, 2, 4; 8, 10, etc.)" (Grand Rapids: Eerdmans, 1964, 274).

had been radically redefined by the gospel. Whether slave or free in this life, they had all been set free from sin; yet having been bought with a price, they had all become slaves of Christ. That is what it meant to be a *Christian*.[13]

The New Testament reflects this perspective, commanding believers to submit to Christ completely, and not just as hired servants or spiritual employees—but as those who belong wholly to Him. We are told to obey Him without question and follow Him without complaint. Jesus Christ is our Master—a fact we acknowledge every time we call Him "Lord." We are His slaves, called to humbly and wholeheartedly obey and honor Him.

We don't hear about that concept much in churches today. In contemporary Christianity the language is anything but slave terminology.[14] It is about success, health, wealth, prosperity, and the pursuit of happiness. We often hear that God loves people unconditionally and wants them to be all *they* want to be. He wants to fulfill every desire, hope, and dream. *Personal* ambition, *personal* fulfillment, *personal* gratification—these have all become part of the language of evangelical Christianity—and part of what it means to have a "personal relationship with Jesus Christ." Instead of teaching the New Testament gospel—where sinners are called to submit to Christ—the

---

13. In a second-century letter from the churches of Lyons and Vienne to the churches of Asia and Phrygia, the anonymous authors began by designating themselves the "slaves of Christ" (Eusebius, *Ecclesiastical History*, 5.1–4). They continued by describing the widespread persecution they had endured, including the martyrdoms that many in their midst had experienced.

14. As Janet Martin Soskice explains, "Talk of the Christian as 'slave of Christ' or 'slave of God' which enjoyed some popularity in the Pauline Epistles and early Church is now scarcely used, despite its biblical warrant, by contemporary Christians, who have little understanding for or sympathy with the institution of slavery and the figures of speech it generates" (*The Kindness of God: Metaphor, Gender, and Religious Language* [New York: Oxford University Press, 2007], 68).

contemporary message is exactly the opposite: Jesus is here to fulfill all *your* wishes. Likening Him to a personal assistant or a personal trainer, many churchgoers speak of a *personal* Savior who is eager to do their bidding and help them in their quest for self-satisfaction or individual accomplishment.

The New Testament understanding of the believer's relationship to Christ could not be more opposite. He is the Master and Owner. We are His possession. He is the King, the Lord, and the Son of God. We are His subjects and His subordinates.

In a word, we are His *slaves*.

Lost in Translation

Scripture's prevailing description of the Christian's relationship to Jesus Christ is the slave/master relationship.[15] But do a casual read through your English New Testament and you won't see it.

The reason for this is as simple as it is shocking: the Greek word for *slave* has been covered up by being mistranslated in almost every English version—going back to both the King James Version and the Geneva Bible that predated it.[16] Though the word *slave* (*doulos* in Greek) appears 124 times in the original text,[17] it is correctly translated

---

15. For example, Rengstorf notes the prominence "in the NT [of] the idea that Christians belong to Jesus as His δοῦλοι [*slaves*], and that their lives are thus offered to Him as the risen and exalted Lord" (*Theological Dictionary of the New Testament*, s.v. "δοῦλος" 2:274).

16. Even earlier, John Wycliffe and William Tyndale rendered the Greek *doulos* with the English word "servant."

17. According to Harris, "this word [*doulos*] occurs 124 times in the New Testament and its compound form *syndoulos* ('fellow-slave') ten times" (*Slave of Christ*, 183). The verb form also occurs an additional eight times.

only once in the King James. Most of our modern translations do only slightly better.[18] It almost seems like a conspiracy.

Instead of translating *doulos* as "slave," these translations consistently substitute the word *servant* in its place. Ironically, the Greek language has at least half a dozen words that can mean *servant*. The word *doulos* is not one of them.[19] Whenever it is used, both in the New Testament and in secular Greek literature, it always and only means *slave*. According to the *Theological Dictionary of the New Testament*, a foremost authority on the meaning of Greek terms in Scripture, the word *doulos* is used exclusively "either to describe the status of a slave or an attitude corresponding to that of a slave."[20] The dictionary continues by noting that

> the meaning is so unequivocal and self-contained that it is superfluous to give examples of the individual terms or to trace the history of the group. . . . [The] emphasis here is always on "serving as a slave." Hence we have a service which is not a matter of choice for the one who renders it, which he has to perform whether he likes it or not, because he is subject as a slave to an alien will, to the will of his owner. [The term stresses] the slave's dependence on his lord.

While it is true that the duties of *slave* and *servant* may overlap to some degree, there is a key distinction between the two: servants are

---

18. Two exceptions to this are E. J. Goodspeed's *The New Testament: An American Translation* (1923) and the Holman Christian Standard Version (2004), both of which consistently render *doulos* as "slave."

19. Cf. Harris, *Slave of Christ*, 183.

20. Rengstorf, *Theological Dictionary of the New Testament*, s.v. "δοῦλος," 2:261.

hired; slaves are *owned.*[21] Servants have an element of freedom in choosing whom they work for and what they do. The idea of servanthood maintains some level of self-autonomy and personal rights. Slaves, on the other hand, have no freedom, autonomy, or rights. In the Greco-Roman world, slaves were considered property, to the point that in the eyes of the law they were regarded as *things* rather than *persons.*[22] To be someone's slave was to be his possession, bound to obey his will without hesitation or argument.[23]

But why have modern English translations consistently mistranslated *doulos* when its meaning is unmistakable in Greek? There are at least two answers to this question. First, given the stigmas attached to slavery in Western society, translators have understandably wanted to avoid any association between biblical teaching and the slave trade of the British Empire and the American Colonial era.[24] For the average

---

21. As Walter S. Wurzburger explains, "To be a slave of God . . . involves more than merely being His servant. Servants retain their independent status. They have only specific duties and limited responsibilities. Slaves, on the other hand, have no rights *vis a vis* their owners, because they are deemed the property of the latter" (*God Is Proof Enough* [New York: Devora Publishing, 2000], 37).

22. Speaking of Roman slavery in particular, Yvon Thébert noted that the slave "was equated with his function and was for his master what the ox was for the poor man: an animated object that he owned. The same idea is a constant in Roman law, where the slave is frequently associated with other parts of a patrimony, sold by the same rules that governed a transfer of a parcel of land or included with tools or animals in a bequest. Above all he was an object, a *res mobilis.* Unlike the waged worker, no distinction was made between his person and his labor" ("The Slave," 138–74 in Andrea Giardina, ed., *The Romans* [Chicago: University of Chicago, 1993], 139).

23. John J. Pilch, under "Slave, Slavery, Bond, Bondage, Oppression," in Donald E. Gowan, ed., *Westminster Theological Wordbook of the Bible* (Louisville, KY: Westminster John Knox Press, 2003), 472, notes that "the Greek noun *doulos* is a sub-domain of the semantic field 'control, rule' and describes someone who is completely controlled by something or someone."

24. Ibid., 474. The author points out that "slavery in the ancient world had practically nothing in common with slavery familiar from New World practice and experience of the eighteenth and nineteenth centuries. It would distort the interpretation of the Bible to impose such an understanding on its books."

reader today, the word *slave* does not conjure up images of Greco-Roman society but rather depicts an unjust system of oppression that was finally ended by parliamentary rule in England and by civil war in the United States. In order to avoid both potential confusion and negative imagery, modern translators have replaced slave language with servant language.

Second, from a historical perspective, in late-medieval times it was common to translate *doulos* with the Latin word *servus*. Some of the earliest English translations, influenced by the Latin version of the Bible, translated *doulos* as "servant" because it was a more natural rendering of *servus*.[25] Added to this, the term *slave* in sixteenth-century England generally depicted someone in physical chains or in prison. Since this is quite different from the Greco-Roman idea of slavery, the translators of early English versions (like the Geneva Bible and the King James) opted for a word they felt better represented Greco-Roman slavery in their culture. That word was *servant*. These early translations continue to have a significant impact on modern English versions.[26]

---

25. Cf. Harris, *Slave of Christ*, 184.

26. For an intriguing look at the early English Bible translators' reticence to translate *doulos* as "slave," see Edwin Yamauchi, "Slaves of God," *Bulletin of the Evangelical Theological Society* 9/1 (Winter 1966): 31–49. Yamauchi shows that by the late thirteenth century, "slavery disappeared from northwestern Europe.... Slavery therefore was known to the 17th-century Englishmen—at least at the beginning of that century—not as an intimate, accepted institution but rather as a remote phenomenon" (p. 41). Their concept of a "servant" was shaped by their knowledge of serfdom—a kind of servitude in which the laborer was bound to the land he worked. Although he was duty-bound to the landowner, his services could only be sold when the land itself was sold. By contrast, "slavery" in their minds evoked "the extreme case of a captive in fetters" (p. 41), an image of cruelty that they understandably wished to avoid. But in so doing they unwittingly diminished the force of the actual biblical expression. In Yamauchi's words, "If we keep in mind what 'slavery' meant to the ancients, and not what it means to us or the 17th-century theorists, we shall gain a heightened understanding of many passages in the New Testament" (43). See also Harris, *Slave of Christ*, 184.

But whatever the rationale behind the change, something significant is lost in translation when *doulos* is rendered "servant" rather than "slave." The gospel is not simply an invitation to become Christ's associate; it is a mandate to become His slave.

Rediscovering This One Hidden Word

The Bible's emphasis on slavery to God is missing from the pages of most English translations. But that which is hidden in our modern versions was a central truth for the apostles and the generations of believers who came after them.

Early Christian leaders, like Ignatius (who died around AD 110) and his coworkers, saw themselves as "fellow slaves" of Christ.[27] Polycarp (c. 69–155) instructed the Philippians, "Bind up your loose robes and serve as God's slaves in reverential fear and truth."[28] *The Shepherd of Hermas* (written in the second century) warns its readers that "there are many [wicked deeds] from which the slave of God must refrain."[29] The fourth-century writer known as Ambrosiaster explained that "the one who is liberated from [the Mosaic Law] 'dies' and lives to God, becoming his slave, purchased by Christ."[30] Augustine (354–430) simply asked his congregation this rhetorical

27. Cf. *Epistle to the Philadelphians*, 3; *Epistle to the Magnesians*, 2; *Epistle to Smyrna*, 12.

28. Polycarp, *Letter to the Philippians*, 2, in Bart D. Ehrman, trans., *The Apostolic Fathers* (Harvard, 2003), 1:335.

29. *Shepherd of Hermas*, Exposition on the Eighth Commandment, 38.3–6, in ibid., II:270. This is just one of several instances in which *Hermas* used the phrase "slave of God."

30. *Corpus Scriptorum Ecclesiasticorum Latinorum*, 81.3: 28.21–23, quoted in Eric Plumer's critical notes on *Augustine's Commentary on Galatians* (New York: Oxford University Press, 2003), 30n153.

question: "Does your Lord not deserve to have you as his trust-worthy slave?"[31] Elsewhere, he rebuked those who would exhibit foolish pride: "You are a creature, acknowledge the Creator; you are a slave, do not disdain the Master."[32] Ancient Bible expositor John Chrysostom (347–407) comforted those who were in physical bondage with these words: "In the things that relate to Christ, both [slaves and masters] are equal: and just as you are the slave of Christ, so also is your master."[33]

Even in more recent history, in spite of the confusion caused by English translations, leading scholars and pastors have recognized the reality of this vital concept.[34] Listen to the words of Charles Spurgeon—the great British preacher of the nineteenth century:

> Where our Authorized [King James] Version softly puts it "servant" it really is "bond-slave." The early saints delighted to count themselves Christ's absolute property, bought by him, owned by him, and wholly at his disposal. Paul even went so far as to rejoice that he had the marks of his Master's brand on him, and he cries, "Let no man trouble me: for I bear in my body the marks of the Lord Jesus." There was the end of all debate: he was the Lord's, and the marks of the scourges, the rods, and the stones were the broad-arrow of the King which marked Paul's body as the property of Jesus the Lord. Now if the saints of old

---

31. Augustine, "Sermon 159," in John E. Rottelle, trans., *Sermons* (Hyde Park, NY: New City Press, 1992), 124.

32. Augustine, *Homilies on the Gospel of John 1–40*, Homily 29, trans. by Edmund Hill (Hyde Park, NY: New City Press, 2009), 495. Capitalization of divine names added.

33. John Chrysostom, *Homilies on First Corinthians*, Homily 19.5–6 (on 1 Cor. 7:22–23), quoted in Schaff, *NPNF*, 12:108–9.

34. See the appendix for additional quotations from recent church history.

time gloried in obeying Christ, I pray that you and I . . . may feel that our first object in life is to obey our Lord.[35]

Scottish pastor Alexander Maclaren, a contemporary of Spurgeon, echoed these same truths:

The true position, then, for a man is to be God's slave. . . . Absolute submission, unconditional obedience, on the slave's part; and on the part of the Master complete ownership, the right of life and death, the right of disposing of all goods and chattels, . . . the right of issuing commandments without a reason, the right to expect that those commandments shall be swiftly, unhesitatingly, punctiliously, and completely performed—these things inhere in our relation to God. Blessed [is] the man who has learned that they do, and has accepted them as his highest glory and the security of his most blessed life! For, brethren, such submission, absolute and unconditional, the blending and the absorption of my own will in His will, is the secret of all that makes manhood glorious and great and happy. . . . [I]n the New Testament these names of slave and owner are transferred to Christians and Jesus Christ.[36]

As these voices from church history make so abundantly clear, our slavery to Christ has radical implications for how we think and live. We have been *bought with a price.* We *belong to Christ.* We are part of a people for *His own possession.* And understanding all of that

---

35. Charles Spurgeon, "Eyes Right," sermon no. 2058, in *The Metropolitan Tabernacle Pulpit* (Pasadena, TX: Pilgrim Publications, 1974), 34:689.

36. Alexander Maclaren, *Expositions of Holy Scripture, the Acts,* commenting on Acts 4:26, 27, 29 (n.p.: BiblioLife, 2007), 148–49.

changes everything about us, starting with our perspective and our priorities.

True Christianity is not about adding Jesus to *my* life. Instead, it is about devoting myself completely to *Him*—submitting wholly to His will and seeking to please Him above all else. It demands dying to self and following the Master, no matter the cost. In other words, to be a Christian is to be Christ's *slave*.

In the pages that follow, we will examine the profound depths of that one hidden word, and in the process we'll discover the life-changing difference it makes.

two

Ancient History,
Timeless Truth

T o fully understand the New Testament's use of slave language, we need to begin with a historical perspective regarding the practice of slavery in the Greco-Roman era.

Slavery was a pervasive social structure in the first-century Roman Empire. In fact, it was so commonplace that its existence as an institution was never seriously questioned by anyone.[1] Slaves of all ages, genders, and ethnicities constituted an important socioeconomic class in ancient Rome. Roughly one-fifth of the empire's population were slaves—totaling as many as twelve million at the outset of the first century AD.[2] Not surprisingly, the entire Roman economy was highly dependent on this sizable pool of both skilled and unskilled labor.

Initially, the Roman slave population came through military

---

1. Along these lines, Dale B. Martin, *Slavery as Salvation* (New Haven: Yale University Press, 1990), 42, wrote, "The institution of slavery itself was never really questioned. Slaves may have resented their bondage, but given the chance they acquired slaves themselves. When freed, they simply moved up a notch in the system, becoming themselves masters and mistresses and pulling their dependents along with them. Almost no one, slaves included, thought to organize society any other way."

2. Murray J. Harris, *Slave of Christ* (Downers Grove, IL: InterVarsity Press, 1999), 34. According to the *International Standard Bible Encyclopedia*, "In the larger cities, such as Rome, Corinth, Ephesus, and Antioch, as many as one-third of the population were legally slaves and another one-third had been slaves earlier in life" (S. S. Bartchy, "Servant; Slave," in Geoffrey W. Bromiley, ed., *ISBE*, vol. 4 [Grand Rapids: Eerdmans, 1988], 420).

conquests. As the empire expanded its borders, it captured huge numbers of people, who were subsequently sold into bondage. But by the first century the majority of slaves inherited their place in society by being born into slavery.[3] Most slaves, then, had never known freedom.

For many slaves, life was difficult—especially for those who worked in the mines or on farms. These "rustic" slaves often lived far away from their city-dwelling owners, under the supervision of a foreman or manager. But there were also many slaves who lived in the cities, working alongside their masters as part of the household. For these "urban" slaves, life was often considerably easier.[4]

Depending on their training and on their masters' needs, slaves functioned in numerous capacities—both inside and outside the home. From teachers to cooks to shopkeepers to doctors, slaves were involved in a wide variety of occupations. From a glance on the street, it would have been difficult to distinguish between slaves and non-slaves. There was essentially no difference in dress; neither were there significant differences in responsibilities. Any line of work a free person might do, a slave might also do.

Household slaves received greater honor than other slaves because they worked more closely with their masters. As members of the household, they were intimately involved in every part of family life— from taking care of the master's children to managing his house or

---

3. S. Scott Bartchy, *First-Century Slavery & 1 Corinthians 7:21* (Eugene, OR: Wipf and Stock Publishers, 2002), 71.

4. Keith Bradley, *Slavery and Society at Rome* (Cambridge, UK: Cambridge University Press, 1994), 58. Bradley explains: "For legal purposes the Romans divided slaves into two categories, those who belonged to the city household, the *familia urbana*, and those who belonged to the rural household, the *familia rustica*. The division was predicated on the assumption that the typical slave-owner maintained a residence or residences in the city stocked with slave domestics and owned landed property in the country that was worked, at least in part, with slave labour."

even administrating his business interests. A wicked slave was a great liability and could cause serious damage to the owner's welfare. But a loyal and hardworking slave was a wonderful asset to his master. The faithful slave could look forward to possibly receiving his freedom one day—a reward that owners often used to motivate their slaves toward full compliance.

Slavery also offered a certain amount of social and economic protection to those whose masters were kind and well respected. Slaves did not have to worry about where their next meal would come from or whether or not they would have a place to stay. Their sole concern was to carry out the interests of their owner. In return, the master cared for their needs. Moreover, if a master was a prestigious or powerful member of the community, such as a government official, his slaves would also be respected because of their relationship to him. A great deal of honor would be given to the slaves of someone highly regarded by Roman society.

That said, we must be careful not to present an overly romantic impression of first-century slavery. To be a slave was to be in someone else's possession, totally subjugated to one's master in everything. Greek philosopher Aristotle defined a slave as a human being who was considered an article of property, someone who belonged completely to another person.[5] Ancient Rome viewed slaves the same way: "The slave had, in principle, no rights, no legal status whatsoever; he was a chattel owned by his master."[6] As a result, a slave "could be owned and

---

5. Aristotle, *Politics*, 1.254a7. W. W. Buckland, in *The Roman Law of Slavery*, noted that "the Roman slave did not possess the attributes which modern analysis regards as essential to personality. Of these, capacity for rights is one, and this the Roman slave had not" (Union, NJ: Lawbook Exchange, 2000, 3).

6. Pierre Grimal, *The Civilization of Rome*, trans. W. S. Maguinness (London: George Allen, 1963), 499.

dealt with like any other piece of property. He was [completely] at the mercy of his owner, without rights."[7]

One's experience as a slave, then, ultimately depended on the demands and goodness of the master. The slaves of abusive and temperamental owners endured a life of misery.[8] But for the slaves of reasonable and even gracious masters, the situation could be exponentially better.[9] As history professor Scott Bartchy explains, "The only thing that slaves in the first century had completely in common was the fact that each of them had an owner. A person's experience in slavery depended almost entirely upon the customs of the owner's family, the business and the particular class of society to which the owner belonged, and the character of the owner himself."[10]

Slavery in the Roman world was as diverse as the number of masters who owned slaves. Whether slaves worked in the fields or in the city; whether they became farmers, household managers, or something else; whether or not they eventually gained their freedom; and whether the quality of their daily existence was positive or negative—everything rested in the hands of the master. Each slave owner

---

7. Michael Grant, *The World of Rome* (New York: World Publishing, 1960), 116.

8. Speaking of the abuses of slavery during this time, Dale B. Martin, in *Slavery as Salvation*, explains that "during the early empire, from the time of Augustus to the end of the second century, millions of human beings must have lived in humiliation and destitution, serving the needs and whims, the pleasures and tempers, of other human beings.... Owners had the right to bind, torture, or kill their slaves. In literature of the time, one continually comes across the opinion that slave life is the worst imaginable" (xiii).

9. Harold Mattingly, *Roman Imperial Civilisation* (New York: Norton & Co., 1971), 177. Mattingly explains that "the evils [and abuses] of slavery might be—in fact were—mitigated by kindliness between masters and slaves born in the house." Along these lines, Peter Jones and Keith Sidwell, eds., in *The World of Rome* (New York: Cambridge University Press, 1997), give examples of the loyalty and friendship that sometimes developed between slaves and kindhearted masters (231–32).

10. Bartchy, *First-Century Slavery & 1 Corinthians 7:21*, 68.

defined the nature of his slaves' lives. For their part, slaves had only one primary objective: to please the master in everything through their loyal obedience to him.

Out of Egypt

It is against this Greco-Roman cultural backdrop that Jesus and the apostles spoke about slavery, using it as an illustration to describe the Christian life. But to fully understand this New Testament metaphor, we also need to briefly consider slavery as it existed in Old Testament Israel.

The Hebrew word for *slave*, *'ebed*, appears in the Old Testament 799 times as a noun and another 290 times as a verb.[11] Though "the most basic idea of *'ebed* is that of a slave,"[12] its fundamental meaning is again lost on the pages of most English translations. The King James Version, for example, never translates *'ebed* as "slave"—opting instead for "servant" or "manservant" the vast majority of the time.[13] But contrast that with the Septuagint, a Greek translation of the Old Testament from before the time of Christ. It translates *'ebed* with

---

11. Claus Westermann, under "עבד," in *Theological Lexicon of the Old Testament*, Ernst Jenni and Claus Westermann, eds., Mark Biddle, trans., vol. 2 (Peabody, MA: Hendrickson, 1997), 822. Westermann notes that "in the social sphere, *'ebed* commonly designates the slave in the Old Testament."

12. Walt Kaiser, "*ābad*" in *Theological Wordbook of the Old Testament*, Gleason L. Archer, R. Laird Harris, and Bruce K. Waltke, eds. (Chicago: Moody, 1980), 2:639.

13. According to Strong's *Lexicon*, the Authorized Version translates the noun form of *'ebed* as "servant" 744 times, "manservant" 23 times, "bondman" 21 times, "bondage" 10 times, "bondservant" once, and "on all sides" once.

forms of *doulos*, or *slave*, more than 400 times![14] The rabbinic scholars who produced the Septuagint understood exactly what *'ebed* meant—which is why slave language was so prominent in that translation. For the Jews of Jesus' day, who were familiar with both the Hebrew Old Testament and the Greek Septuagint, the Bible's repeated use of slave imagery would have been impossible to miss.

Slavery was part of Israel's history from her earliest days as a nation. Even before Isaac was born, in Genesis 15, God revealed to Abraham that his descendants would one day experience great suffering as slaves in a foreign land. A preview of the coming affliction came only three generations later when Abraham's great-grandson Joseph was sold into bondage by his brothers. But what Joseph's brothers intended for evil, God orchestrated for good—exalting the former slave to a place of political power and using him to save the lives of millions from famine. In the end, Joseph was reconciled to his brothers and reunited with his father, Jacob. His entire family even moved down to Egypt, where they settled in a region called Goshen.

Though initially welcomed with honor, the descendants of Jacob (or Israel, as he was renamed in Genesis 35) were eventually enslaved by the Egyptians. The first chapter of Exodus explains that

> a new king arose over Egypt, who did not know Joseph. . . . So [the Egyptians] appointed taskmasters over [the Israelites] to afflict them

---

14. The Septuagint (LXX) uses *doulos* to translate the noun form of *'ebed* 314 times. Additionally, the verb form of *doulos* (*douleuo*) is used to translate the verb form of *'ebed* 114 times. In all, the LXX translates *'ebed* with some form of *doulos* 428 times. Cf. Eugene Carpenter, "עבד," in William Van Gemeran, ed., *New International Dictionary of Old Testament Theology and Exegesis* (Grand Rapids: Zondervan, 1997), 3:306. (Hereafter, *New International Dictionary of Old Testament Theology and Exegesis* will be referred to as *NIDOTTE*.)

with hard labor. . . . The Egyptians compelled the sons of Israel to labor rigorously; and they made their lives bitter with hard labor in mortar and bricks and at all kinds of labor in the field, all their labors which they rigorously imposed on them. (vv. 8, 11, 13–14)

When the Israelites cried out to God for help, He delivered them in a way that was as spectacular as it was supernatural. The accounts of Moses' life, the burning bush, the ten plagues, the Passover, and the parting of the Red Sea are all Sunday school classics. But we must not let our familiarity with the stories detract from the staggering wonder of what took place. Egypt, the world power of its day, was systematically dismantled under the breathtaking wrath of God—as He gloriously put His majesty on display and set His people free.

But the exodus from Egypt did not give the Israelites complete autonomy. Rather, it issued them into a different kind of bondage. Those who had once been the property of Pharaoh became the Lord's possession. "You shall be My own possession among all the peoples," God told them as they camped at the foot of Mount Sinai (Ex. 19:5). Later He told Moses, "For the Israelites are My slaves. They are My slaves I brought out of the land of Egypt; I am the LORD your God" (Lev. 25:55 HCSB). The Hebrew people had been delivered from one master in order to serve another. God would be their sovereign King, and they would be His loyal subjects. The Exodus did not rescue them from slavery altogether, but only from slavery to Pharaoh. Now they were the slaves of God: "The Exodus represented a historical event that formed the basis on which Israel understood itself as the slaves of God. Included in this understanding was the obligation to serve God in loyal obedience and to reject all others.... To call oneself an Israelite was the same as calling oneself a slave of God."[15]

Sadly, throughout Israel's history, the Jews frequently forgot that He was their Master. Instead of obeying and honoring Him alone, they repeatedly flirted with idolatry and rebellion against the Lord. God responded by allowing the surrounding nations to conquer and oppress them. If His people were unwilling to be His slaves, they would once again become the slaves of their enemies.[16]

The book of Judges details Israel's repeated failures in this regard. Yet in spite of the nation's unfaithfulness, God remained faithful. He was always quick to deliver His people when they cried out to Him in heartfelt repentance.

Even after the monarchy was established in Israel, the people continued to resist slavery to God in a true-hearted way. The nation's idolatrous path eventually led to its complete removal from the promised land, culminating in the Babylonian exile. Having been rescued from Egypt centuries before, God's people again found themselves in wholesale captivity.[17] And once again, the Lord would deliver them (cf. Ezra 9:9).

Nehemiah—the man God used to bring a remnant of Jews back to the promised land—understood this very point. When he asked the Lord for forgiveness and deliverance on behalf of the people, he began his prayer with these words:

---

15. John Byron, *Slavery Metaphors in Early Judaism and Pauline Christianity* (Tubingen, Germany: J. C. B. Mohr, 2003), 50–51. Also see I. A. H. Combes, *The Metaphor of Slavery in the Writings of the Early Church* (Sheffield, England: Sheffield Academic Press, 1998), 43–44.

16. Cf. Lev. 26:13–17; Deut. 28:58–68; 2 Chr. 12:8.

17. Eugene Carpenter, in *NIDOTTE* ("עבד," 3:306), shows the connection between the Babylonian captivity and the Exodus: "In a great reversal of God's deliverance in the Exodus, he will enslave (*'bd*) Israel to her enemies (Jer. 17:4)."

I beseech You, O Lord God of heaven, the great and awesome God, who preserves the covenant and lovingkindness for those who love Him and keep His commandments, let Your ear now be attentive and Your eyes open to hear the prayer of Your [slave (*'ebed*)] which I am praying before You now, day and night, on behalf of the sons of Israel Your [slaves (*'ebedi*)], confessing the sins of the sons of Israel which we have sinned against You; I and my father's house have sinned. (Neh. 1:5–6)[18]

Nehemiah ended his prayer by recalling the words of Moses and asking God to again save the people whom, centuries before, He had "redeemed by [His] great power and by [His] strong hand" (v. 10).

From the Exodus through the Exile and beyond, Israel's corporate identity as God's slaves was an integral part of the nation's history. Many of Israel's heroes, including Abraham, Moses, Joshua, David, Elijah, and the prophets, are specifically referred to as His slaves.[19]

But the Old Testament understanding of slavery was not solely a matter of national identity. The institution also existed as part of everyday life in ancient Israel. Though fellow Israelites could sell themselves into debt slavery due to financial insolvency, they were to be treated as hired servants under the Mosaic law (cf. Lev. 25:35–43).[20]

---

18. The word for "slave" in these verses is *'ebed* in Hebrew, and is translated with forms of *doulos* (or "slave") in the Greek Septuagint. Thus, it is best rendered in English as "slave," not as "servant."

19. Cf. Judg. 2:8; 1 Kings 18:36; 2 Kings 18:12; Pss. 89:3, 105:42; Isa. 48:20; Ezek. 38:17; Dan. 9:11. These verses are translated with forms of *doulos* in the Septuagint. Karl Heinrich Rengstorf, under "Doúlos," in *Theological Dictionary of the New Testament Abridged in One Volume* (Gerhard Kittel and Gerhard Friedrich, eds.; Geoffrey Bromiley, trans. [Grand Rapids: Eerdmans, 1985], 183), adds that the verb form of "*douleúein* in the LXX is the most common term for the service of God, not just in isolated acts, but in total commitment. . . . For this reason *doúloi* is a title of honor when conferred on such outstanding figures as [those listed above]. The opposite of *douleúein* is disobedience."

20. J. Albert Harrill, under "Slave" in *Eerdmans Dictionary of the Bible* (Grand Rapids:

Non-Jewish slaves, on the other hand, "were regarded and treated as chattels or movable property (Lev. 25:44–46),"[21] having been obtained through capture, purchase, or birth to slave parents. Under the Law, these domestic slaves were guaranteed certain protections, and therefore were treated better than in other Ancient Near Eastern societies.[22] Nevertheless, as in Rome, they were primarily "considered a financial investment and unproductive or disobedient slaves could expect punishment (Ex. 21:20–21)."[23]

Though the two institutions were by no means identical, the slavery of Old Testament Israel shared certain similarities with that of first-century Rome. In particular, foreign slaves could be purchased and therefore owned as property; they were fully subject to the will of the master; they were rewarded or punished on the basis of their performance; and they could be held as slaves indefinitely.[24] Like all slaves in the ancient world, their lives were characterized by "the ideas of total

---

Eerdmans, 2000), notes that at times these Mosaic safeguards were ignored. He has written, "Although designed to curtail and perhaps even to end debt-slavery, these Deuteronomistic laws apparently went unheeded, as debt-slavery of fellow Hebrews continued to be common throughout the biblical period (2 Kgs. 4:1; Amos 2:6; 8:6; Mic. 2:9)" (David Noel Freedman, ed., 1232).

21. Harris, *Slave of Christ*, 28.

22. Cf. Lev. 25:6; Ex. 20:10; 21:26–27. Harris notes that "in comparison with other Ancient Near Eastern societies, Israel's regulations governing slavery (principally in Exod. 21, Lev. 25 and Deut. 15) are more humane" (*Slave of Christ*, 28).

23. John Byron, *Slavery Metaphors*, 40–41. Byron notes that debt slavery, temple slavery, and state slavery were also practiced in ancient Israel, in addition to domestic slavery.

24. William J. Webb, "Slavery," *Dictionary for Theological Interpretation of the Bible*, ed. Kevin Vanhoozer (Grand Rapids: Baker Academic, 2005), 751. Webb notes that in ancient Israel, foreign slaves were considered property (Ex. 12:44; 21:20–21, 32; Lev. 22:11); they were not released every seven years (Lev. 25:39–46); and their owners were permitted to beat them, provided they did not kill them (Ex. 21:20–21). I. A. H. Combes further notes that "the Hebrew slave was, by law, to be released after a set period of time, while the Gentile slave might be held in perpetuity" (*The Metaphor of Slavery*, 38).

dependence, the forfeiture of autonomy and the sense of belonging wholly to another."[25]

The Master's Men

When the apostles used slave imagery, both in their preaching and in writing the New Testament, they were fully aware of what it meant in terms of both Jewish history and Roman culture.[26] From the standpoint of Israel's history, to be a slave of God was to identify oneself with those who stood at Mount Sinai and with noble intentions proclaimed, "All the words which the LORD has spoken we will do!" (Ex. 24:3). Moreover, it was to be aligned with notable men of faith, such as Abraham, Moses, David, and the prophets—spiritual leaders who exemplified wholehearted submission to the will and word of God. From the standpoint of first-century culture, slavery served as an apt picture of the believer's relationship to Christ—one of complete submission and subjugation to the master. In both cases, to be a slave was to be under the complete authority of someone else. It meant rejecting personal autonomy and embracing the will of another. The concept required no great explanation because slavery was commonplace and had been for many centuries.

---

25. Harris, *Slave of Christ*, 45.

26. For example, noting the dual influences of Old Testament theology and Greco-Roman culture on Paul's thinking, Peter Garnsey explains that "Paul was a Christian theologian steeped in the Jewish scriptures and law. He also drew ideas from classical philosophy, even if second-hand and in an attenuated form. These influences, when fused with Paul's own historical experience and perception of the social and ideological context, produced the distinctive mix which is Pauline slave theory" (*Ideas of Slavery from Aristotle to Augustine* [New York: Cambridge University Press, 1996], 186).

When the apostle Paul referred to himself as a "slave of Christ" and a "slave of God,"[27] his readers knew exactly what he meant. Of course, this did not make the claim any less shocking. In a Greco-Roman context, such as the cities to which Paul wrote, personal freedom was prized, slavery was denigrated, and self-imposed slavery was scorned and despised.[28] But for Paul, whose sole ambition was to be pleasing to Christ, there could not have been a more fitting self-designation.[29] His life revolved around the Master. Nothing else—including his own personal agenda—mattered.

The other New Testament writers echoed Paul's heartfelt devotion to the Lord. James did not boast about being Jesus' half-brother but instead called himself "James, a slave of God and of the Lord Jesus Christ" (James 1:1 HCSB). Later in his letter, James instructed his readers with these familiar words: "Come now, you who say, 'Today or tomorrow we will go to such and such a city, and spend a year there and engage in business and make a profit.' . . . Instead, you ought to say, 'If the Lord wills, we will live and also do this or that'" (4:13, 15). Such language draws heavily on the slave/master relationship. Slaves could not go and do whatever they wished. They were bound to follow the will of the master.

Peter, Jude, and John all likewise designated themselves as slaves

---

27. See Romans 1:1; Galatians 1:10; Philippians 1:1; Titus 1:1. Dale B. Martin, in *Slavery as Salvation*, has an important explanation about how Paul's use of "slaves of Christ" was based not solely on an Old Testament Israelite understanding of slavery to God, but also (and largely) on a Greco-Roman understanding of slavery (xvi).

28. Karl Heinrich Rengstorf wrote, "Greeks have a strong sense of freedom. Personal dignity consists of freedom. There is thus a violent aversion to bondage. Service may be rendered to the state, but by free choice. Slavery is scorned and rejected" (*Theological Dictionary of the New Testament Abridged*, s.v. "Doúlos," 183).

29. Cf. 2 Cor. 4:5; 5:9.

bound to do the work of the Lord.[30] These men were companions of our Savior and the leaders of the early church. By all accounts, they might rightly be considered the spiritually elite. Yet they were happy to identify themselves as slaves.

When we survey the New Testament, we quickly find that the term "slave of Christ" was not reserved for low-level believers or spiritual neophytes. The apostles eagerly embraced the title for themselves and also used it to refer to others in ministry.[31] It is not surprising, then, to find slave imagery used frequently throughout their epistles in reference to the Christian life. Slavery was a fitting metaphor, as one historian explains:

> The experience of enslavement was [a] perfect [illustration] for an ancient audience. Like a slave, the [Christian] convert experienced the violent psychological force of personal upheaval, the social dishonor of turning away from one's family and traditional culture, and the natal alienation of losing one's whole past identity—getting a new name, having to learn a new language and worldview, and forming new kinship relations.[32]

The word *doulos*, or *slave*, is even used throughout the book of Revelation to describe the believer's eternal relationship to the Lord. At both the beginning and the end of the book, we are told that this

---

30. Cf. 2 Peter 1:1; Jude 1; Rev. 1:1.

31. Cf. Acts 4:29; 16:17; Col. 1:7; 4:12; 2 Tim. 2:24.

32. J. Albert Harrill, *Slaves in the New Testament* (Minneapolis: Fortress Press, 2006), 32. Earlier, Harrill explained that "the figure of the slave provides a powerful and compelling idiom through which to articulate Christian community formation and self-definition precisely because early Christians shared with wider 'pagan' society the same set of cultural assumptions, literary tropes, and social stereotyping of the slave" (31–32).

revelation was given by God "to show His slaves what must quickly take place" (Rev. 1:1 HCSB). In Revelation 7:3, the converts who comprise the 144,000 are called "the slaves of our God" (HCSB). The prophets are similarly referred to with the word *doulos* in Revelation 10:7, as are the martyrs in Revelation 19:2. But it is not until the end of the book that *all* believers are described as the slaves of God in a collective sense. Revelation 22:3–4, a passage that depicts the glories of the eternal state, says this: "There will no longer be any curse; and the throne of God and of the Lamb will be in it, and His bond-servants [*douloi*; literally, *slaves*] will serve Him; they will see His face, and His name will be on their foreheads." The glorious reality is that, for all of eternity as His slaves, you and I and every other believer from all of human history will joyfully worship and exalt our heavenly Master—the King of kings and the Lord of lords.

three

The Good and Faithful Slave

The truth of God's Word is always countercultural, and the notion of becoming a slave is certainly no exception. In fact, it is difficult to imagine a concept more distasteful to modern sensibilities than that of slavery. Western society, in particular, places a high premium on personal liberty and freedom of choice. So, to present the good news in terms of a slave/master relationship runs contrary to everything our culture holds dear. Such an approach is controversial, confrontational, and politically incorrect. Yet that is precisely the way the Bible speaks about what it means to follow Christ.

Slavery in the Teaching of Jesus

In presenting the gospel through the lens of slavery, we are following the example of Jesus Himself. Our Lord neither advocated nor denounced the institution of slavery as it existed in His day. But He found it an apt analogy to illustrate certain truths about the gospel and the kingdom of God. As one scholar explains:

> Jesus routinely evoked the figure of the slave in his teachings. . . . For modern commentators, slaves and slavery have often been, first and foremost, metaphorical. For Jesus, slaves and slavery were part of the

fabric of everyday life. Jesus relied on the figure of the slave in his discourse not because the trope of slavery was part of his philosophical or rhetorical inheritance, but because slaves were ubiquitous in the world in which he lived: cooking food, harvesting grain, and absorbing blows.[1]

Jesus drew many of His illustrations and parables from the slave world of His day.[2] Slaves might be working in the fields, collecting produce from a vineyard, inviting guests to a wedding, overseeing household duties, or assisting with special occasions for the family.[3] But whatever the specific depiction, Christ repeatedly used slave imagery as the best analogy to clarify profound spiritual realities.

From the teaching of Jesus[4] we learn that slaves are not greater than their master; neither are they privy to the master's plans. They are accountable to the master for how they use his resources, even in his absence. They are also liable for how they treat their fellow slaves and are subject to considerable punishment if they are unmerciful to others. Slaves are expected to obey and honor their master without complaint, though the faithful slave will be honored for his diligent

---

1. Jennifer A. Glancy, *Slavery in Early Christianity* (Minneapolis: Fortress Press, 2006), 129. In the Gospels, for example, both a Gentile centurion (Luke 7:2–10) and the Jewish high priest (Matt. 26:51; Mark 14:47; Luke 22:50; John 18:10, 17–18, 26) are noted as being slave owners.

2. Karl Heinrich Rengstorf wrote, "In the parables this is also true, but the total commitment of *douloi* and the total claim of the *kýrios* serve here to illustrate the unconditional lordship of God and the unconditional responsibility of believers to him" (Gerhard Kittel and Gerhard Friedrich, eds.; Geoffrey Bromiley, trans., *Theological Dictionary of the New Testament Abridged in One Volume* [Grand Rapids: Eerdmans, 1985], s.v. "Doúlos," 184).

3. Cf. Matt. 13:27–28; 21:34–36; 22:3–10; 24:45; Mark 12:2–4; 13:34; Luke 14:17–23; 15:22; 20:10–11.

4. Cf. Matt. 10:24; 18:23, 26–33; 24:45–50; 25:14–30; Luke 6:40; 12:37–47; 17:7–10; 19:13–22; John 13:16; 15:15–20.

service. Moreover, slaves can expect to be treated by outsiders the way their master is treated. If the master is treated with contempt, slaves should expect their treatment to be no better.

Jesus also used slave language to define the reality of what it means to follow Him. Discipleship, like slavery, entails a life of total self-denial, a humble disposition toward others, a wholehearted devotion to the Master alone, a willingness to obey His commands in everything, an eagerness to serve Him even in His absence, and a motivation that comes from knowing He is well pleased.[5] Though they were once the slaves of sin, Christ's followers receive spiritual freedom and rest for their souls through their saving relationship with Him.[6]

Against the historical backdrop of slavery, our Lord's call to self-sacrifice becomes that much more vivid.[7] A slave's life was one of complete surrender, submission, and service to the master—and the people of Jesus' day would have immediately recognized the parallel. Christ's invitation to follow Him was an invitation to that same kind of life.

Making It Personal

Throughout the New Testament, believers are repeatedly called to embrace the perspective of those who belong to Christ and therefore

---

5. Cf. Matt. 24:44–46; 25:21; Mark 10:44; Luke 6:46; 12:37; 14:26–33; 16:13; John 14:15, 21.

6. See John 8:34, 36, and Matt. 11:28–30.

7. As Michael Card explains, "'Take up your cross and follow me.' These are slave words from Jesus, for crucifixion was a slave's death (Matthew 10:38; 16:24). . . . 'Take up my yoke,' Jesus invites. Take your place alongside others who are slaving for me and the gospel" (*A Better Freedom* [Downers Grove, IL: InterVarsity, 2009], 23).

lovingly submit to Him as Master. That kind of perspective has serious implications for how we, as believers, think and act. Consider, for example, the following five parallels between biblical Christianity and first-century slavery.

Exclusive Ownership

As we saw in chapter 2, Roman law considered slaves to be "property in the absolute control of an owner."[8] Hired servants, like modern employees, could choose their masters and quit if they wanted to do so, but slaves had no such choice.[9] Whether they were sold into slavery or born into it, slaves belonged entirely to those who owned them.

The New Testament picks up on this theme as it explains both the believer's sinful past and present relationship to Christ. Though we were born as slaves of sin, having inherited an enslaved state from Adam, we were purchased by Christ through His death on the cross.[10] We were bought with a price; therefore, we are no longer under the authority of sin. Instead we are under the exclusive ownership of God.[11] Christ is our new Master.[12] As Paul told the Romans, "Thanks

---

8. Thomas Wiedemann, *Greek & Roman Slavery* (New York: Routledge, 1988), 15.

9. S. Scott Bartchy has noted this distinction between slaves and freedmen: "Of course, if the freedman did not enter a restrictive contract as the price of his freedom, he had an advantage over the slave in that he could give notice that he was quitting" (*First-Century Slavery & 1 Corinthians 7:21* [Eugene, OR: Wipf and Stock Publishers, 2002], 74).

10. Rom. 5:18–19; Eph. 2:1–3; cf. 1 Peter 1:18–19; Rev. 5:9.

11. Rom. 6:14; 1 Cor. 7:23.

12. Cf. Leland Ryken, James C. Wilhoit, Tremper Longman III, eds., "Slave, Slavery," *The Dictionary of Biblical Imagery* (Downers Grove, IL: InterVarsity Press, 1998), 797. The article notes that "from the biblical perspective every person is subject to slavery, either to sin or to God." John J. Pilch echoes that thought in "Slave, Slavery, Bond, Bondage, Oppression." He observes that "in the Bible, no one is ever really 'free' but rather always a slave of someone.

be to God that though you were slaves of sin, you became obedient from the heart to that form of teaching to which you were committed, and having been freed from sin, you became slaves of righteousness" (Rom. 6:17–18).

As Christians, we are part of "a people for His own possession" (Titus 2:14), having joined the multitude of those who "belong to Christ Jesus" (Gal. 5:24) and who worship Him as our "Master in heaven" (Col. 4:1). Just as first-century slaves would receive new names from their earthly masters,[13] so will we each be given a new name from Christ. He Himself promised in Revelation 3:12, to the one who overcomes, "I will write on him the name of My God, and the name of the city of My God, the new Jerusalem, which comes down out of heaven from My God, and My new name." Believers in the eternal state will serve the Lord as His slaves forever, "and His name will be on their foreheads" (Rev. 22:4). The imagery is inescapable, as one commentator explains: "'To write the name upon' anything is a common figurative expression in Hebrew to denote taking absolute possession of, and making completely one's own."[14] We will receive Christ's name because we will forever be His exclusive possession.

Israel accepted with gratitude its new status as 'slaves of God.' Paul suggests the same for Christians (Donald E. Gowan, ed., *Westminster Theological Wordbook of the Bible* [Louisville: Westminster John Knox Press, 2003], 475–76).

13. William Blair, *An Inquiry into the State of Slavery amongst the Romans* (Edinburgh: Thomas Clark, 1833; repr., Detroit: Negro History Press, 1970), 116. Blair explains that "owners, on first acquiring slaves, gave them what appellatives they thought fit: those for bought slaves being, most commonly, taken from the name of their country, or birth-place; or from the names chiefly used there; or else from the place of purchase: and slaves, who had been taken in war, were, not infrequently, named after their captors."

14. A. Plummer, *The Revelation of St. John the Divine*, *The Pulpit Commentary* (repr., Grand Rapids: Eerdmans, 1978), 113.

Complete Submission

Being a slave not only meant belonging to someone else; it also meant being always available to obey that person in every way. The slave's sole duty was to carry out the master's wishes, and the faithful slave was eager to do so without hesitation or complaint. After all, "slaves know no law but their master's word; they have no rights of their own; they are absolute possessions of their master; and they are bound to give their master unquestioning obedience."[15]

Building on this imagery, the New Testament repeatedly calls believers to faithfully obey the Master. As one author explains:

As Christ is Lord, so the Christian is slave, even bondslave, owing unquestioning obedience. Paul explicitly compares spiritual with literal slavery (e.g. Colossians 3:22–24), speaks of slave-marks and seals of Christ's possession, and works out in detail the conception of the Christian as purchased, belonging to his Lord: "Ye are not your own, ye are bought with a price." To be alive at all "means fruitful labor"— the slave exists only to work! (1 Corinthians 6:19, 20, Philippians 1:22) So represented, consecration is complete moral submission to Christ's absolute claim and ownership.[16]

Submission to the lordship of Christ—a heart attitude that works itself out in obedience to Him—is the defining mark of those who are genuinely converted. First John 2:3 is explicit in this regard:

---

15. William Barclay, *The Letters of James and Peter* (Louisville: Westminster John Knox Press, 2003), 39.

16. Reginald E. O. White, *Christian Ethics* (Macon, GA: Mercer University Press, 1994), 166. White is a former principal of the Baptist Theological College of Scotland.

"By this we know that we have come to know Him, if we keep His commandments."

As His slaves, we are expected "to obey Jesus Christ" (1 Peter 1:2), "to present [our] bodies a living and holy sacrifice, acceptable to God, which is [our] spiritual service of worship" (Rom. 12:1), and to "keep His commandments and do the things that are pleasing in His sight" (1 John 3:22). "You have been bought with a price," Paul told the Corinthians, "therefore glorify God in your body" (1 Cor. 6:20). And later, "Whether, then, you eat or drink or whatever you do, do all to the glory of God" (10:31).

Those who claim to belong to Christ but persist in patterns of disobedience betray the reality of that profession. The apostle John explained: "If we say that we have fellowship with Him and yet walk in the darkness, we lie and do not practice the truth" (1 John 1:6). Such is especially true of false teachers, whom the New Testament describes as "slaves of corruption" (2 Peter 2:19) and as "slaves, not of our Lord Christ but of their own appetites" (Rom. 16:18). They are "ungodly persons who turn the grace of our God into licentiousness and deny our only Master and Lord, Jesus Christ" (Jude 4; cf. 2 Peter 2:1). The true man of God, by contrast, is "the Lord's slave" making himself "useful to the Master, prepared for every good work" (2 Tim. 2:24, 21 HCSB).

Singular Devotion

The life of a slave in New Testament times may have been difficult, but it was relatively simple. Slaves had only one primary concern: to carry out the will of the master. In areas where they were given direct commands, they were required to obey. In areas where no direct command was given, they were to find ways to please the master as best they could.

That kind of focused dedication marking first-century slavery also characterizes biblical Christianity. Like slaves, we are to be fully devoted to our Master alone. Our greatest concern is summed up in the words of Christ: "You shall love the Lord your God with all your heart, with all your soul, with all your mind, and with all your strength" (Mark 12:30 NKJV). Such exclusive devotion makes it impossible to serve God and other masters at the same time. We cannot simultaneously serve God and money, worship the true God and idols, or live according to the Spirit and the flesh.[17]

In all things we are to do "that which is pleasing in His sight" (Heb. 13:21). Such was the motivation behind Paul's words to the Corinthians, "Therefore we also have as our ambition, whether at home or absent, to be pleasing to Him" (2 Cor. 5:9). Believers are "to please Him in all respects" (Col. 1:10), "to walk and please God" (1 Thess. 4:1), and to do that which is "acceptable to God" (Rom. 14:18). We are called to seek His glory in everything we do, longing to conduct ourselves in a manner worthy of His name.[18] Ultimately, the only thing that matters is the Master's approval and reward. For the faithful slave, that is a sufficient motivation.

Total Dependence

As part of the master's household, slaves were completely dependent on their owners for the basic necessities of life, including food and shelter. Meals usually consisted of corn, though grain or bread was sometimes given instead. "Along with corn or bread, salt and oil were commonly allowed. Neither meat nor vegetables formed a part

---

17. Cf. Matt. 6:24; Rom. 7:5–6; 6:11–18; 1 Thess. 1:9.

18. Cf. 1 Cor. 10:31; Col. 2:12; 3:17; 1 Thess. 2:12.

of the regular diet of slaves; but they occasionally got a small quantity of vinegar, and salt fish, or olives, when figs and other fruits were not abundant."[19] With regard to shelter, domestic slaves usually lived with their masters, either in separate slave quarters or—in the case of smaller households—wherever there was available space.[20] Though basic from a modern perspective, such provisions were generally adequate. Moreover, they gave slaves a significant advantage over non-slaves. Unlike free persons, slaves did not have to worry about finding something to eat or somewhere to sleep. Because their needs were met, they could focus entirely on serving the master.

Again, the parallels to the Christian life are striking. As believers, we can focus on the things God has called us to do, trusting Him to meet our needs. "Do not worry then, saying, 'What will we eat?' or 'What will we drink?' or 'What will we wear for clothing?'" Jesus told His followers. "Your heavenly Father knows that you need all these things. But seek first His kingdom and His righteousness, and all these things will be added to you" (Matt. 6:31–33). Those who make pleasing God their highest priority can be confident that He will take care of them.[21]

No one understood this principle better than the apostle Paul. As a "slave of Christ," he had given up everything in order to serve His Master. His ministry was not an easy one, humanly speaking. He had been repeatedly beaten, imprisoned, endangered, and threatened with

19. Blair, *An Inquiry into the State of Slavery*, 95.

20. See Jennifer A. Glancy, *Slavery in Early Christianity*, 45.

21. Cf. Ryken, Wilhoit, and Longman, "Slave, Slavery," *The Dictionary of Biblical Imagery*, 798. The article notes that "the slave-master relation parallels ours with God because we are called to be accountable to him. . . . [By the same token,] He also assumes responsibility for us: 'As the eyes of slaves look to the hand of their master . . . so our eyes look to the LORD our God, till he shows us his mercy' (Ps 123:2 NIV)."

death. Yet in spite of it all, God always provided Paul with all that he needed to faithfully accomplish his ministry. "Be anxious for nothing," he wrote to the Philippians, "but in everything by prayer and supplication . . . let your requests be made known to God" (4:6). Later in that chapter, he explained that he had learned the secret of being content, no matter his circumstances. Consequently, he could exclaim, "I can do all things through Him who strengthens me" (v. 13). Paul's contentment came both from relying on Christ completely and also from rightly assessing his needs. As he explained to Timothy, "If we have food and covering, with these we shall be content" (1 Tim. 6:8).

Based on a lifetime of trusting his Master, Paul could confidently tell the Philippians, "My God will supply all your needs according to His riches in glory in Christ Jesus" (4:19). He had similarly told the Corinthians, "God is able to make all grace abound to you, so that always having all sufficiency in everything, you may have an abundance for every good deed" (2 Cor. 9:8). Paul himself relied daily on Christ, resting in God's promise to him: "My grace is sufficient for you, for power is perfected in weakness" (2 Cor. 12:9). Even in the midst of seemingly dire circumstances, Paul remained confident and thankful.[22] Simply knowing he was in the Master's care made it possible to face any difficulty. As he wrote to the believers in Rome:

> Who will separate us from the love of Christ? Will tribulation, or distress, or persecution, or famine, or nakedness, or peril, or sword? . . . I am convinced that neither death, nor life, nor angels, nor principalities, nor things present, nor things to come, nor powers, nor height, nor depth, nor any other created thing, will be able to separate us

---

22. Cf. Acts 16:25; 1 Thess. 5:18.

from the love of God, which is in Christ Jesus our Lord. (Rom. 8:35, 38–39)

Paul could list all of these potential threats from his own personal experience.[23] He knew firsthand that none of them could sever his Master's love for him.

Personal Accountability

In everything they did, first-century slaves were entirely accountable to their owners. Ultimately, the master's evaluation was the only one that mattered. If the master was pleased, the slave would benefit accordingly. A lifetime of faithfulness might even be rewarded with eventual manumission, or freedom. But if the master was displeased, the slave could expect appropriate discipline, often as severe as flogging. More extreme punishments including "crucifixion, the breaking of bones, amputations, hot tar, restraining collars and the rack"[24] were rare but permissible under Roman law. Such a weighty system of rewards and punishments provided powerful stimulation for slaves to work hard and do well.

Believers likewise are to be impelled by the realization that one day they will stand before Christ. The desire to please the Master is heightened by the knowledge that "each one of us will give an account of himself to God" (Rom. 14:12). "For we must all appear before the judgment seat of Christ, so that each one may be recompensed for his deeds in the body, according to what he has done" (2 Cor. 5:10). Each of us, like the diligent slave pictured in Matthew 25, longs to hear the Lord

---

23. For a list of some of the trials Paul endured for Christ's sake, see 2 Corinthians 11:23–33.

24. Murray J. Harris, *Slave of Christ* (Downers Grove, IL: InterVarsity Press, 1999), 42.

say those joyous words, "Well done, good and faithful slave. . . . Enter into the joy of your Master" (vv. 21, 23). We take heart in knowing that all who persevere in faithfulness will receive "the crown of righteousness, which the Lord, the righteous Judge, will award . . . to all who have loved His appearing" (2 Tim. 4:8).

In the context of the early church, a significant number of believers also would have been Roman slaves. Paul encouraged these Christians by reminding them that in serving their earthly masters, they were ultimately serving the Lord. In such cases, motivation for obedience went beyond any earthly incentive to heavenly reward. To the slaves in Colossae, Paul wrote, "Slaves, in all things obey those who are your masters on earth, not with external service, as those who merely please men, but with sincerity of heart, fearing the Lord. Whatever you do, do your work heartily, as for the Lord rather than for men, knowing that from the Lord you will receive the reward of the inheritance. It is the Lord Christ whom you serve" (Col. 3:22–24; cf. Eph. 6:5–8).

Christian masters also needed to remember that they had a heavenly Master. Paul continued by exhorting the Colossian slave owners with these words: "Masters, grant to your slaves justice and fairness, knowing that you too have a Master in heaven" (Col. 4:1; cf. Eph. 6:9).

Remembering the Master in heaven was a powerful force for the earliest Christians—whether slave or free. It should motivate us as well. Whether or not our faithfulness is rewarded in this life doesn't really matter. One day we will stand before Christ to be recompensed in full. What a glorious day that will be! In the words of Charles Spurgeon:

[On that day,] the Lord will grant unto his people an abundant reward for all that they have done. Not that they deserve any reward, but that God first gave them grace to do good works, then took their good works as evidence of a renewed heart, and then gave them a reward for what they had done. Oh, what a bliss it will be to hear it said, "Well done, good and faithful servant,"—and to find that you have worked for Christ when nobody knew it, to find that Christ took stock of it all,—to you that served the Lord under misrepresentation, to find that the Lord Jesus cleared the chaff away from the wheat, and knew that you were one of his precious ones. For him, then, to say, "Enter into the joy of thy Lord," oh, what a bliss will it be to you.[25]

---

25. Charles Spurgeon, "The Great Assize," sermon no. 1076, *Metropolitan Tabernacle Pulpit* (Pasadena, TX: Pilgrim Publications, 1984), 18:587.

four

The Lord and Master
(Part 1)

T o this point, we have considered the biblical metaphor of slavery to Christ from the standpoint of the slave, focusing on the word *doulos* and its implications for the Christian life. In this chapter, we will turn our attention to the other side of the slave/master relationship—seeking to understand what the Bible means when it calls Jesus Christ our "Lord" and "Master" (or *kyrios* in Greek). We will begin by considering the truth that He is the Lord and Master over His church. Then, in the next two chapters, we will broaden our study to consider Christ's rightful place as Master over every person and thing that exists in the universe.

◄─►

It was the morning of July 6, 1415. The greatest preacher of his generation—and one of the foremost in all of church history—stood on trial once again. This time, however, would be his last.

He had already endured more than seven months of tortuous imprisonment. Though he had been promised safe passage to and from his trial, he was arrested and thrown in prison shortly after he arrived. At first, he was cast into a dark, dismal dungeon that was near the sewer. The conditions were so rancid that he soon became violently ill and likely would have died if he had not been relocated. But subsequent quarters were hardly any better. He soon found himself confined to a high castle tower, where his feet were constantly fettered and his hands chained to the wall every night.

Though interrogated on several occasions, he was never given an adequate opportunity to publicly defend himself or clarify his views. The official proceedings against him, which began on June 5, consisted of nothing more than a mock trial. When he attempted to explain his writings, his voice was drowned out by the angry shouts of his accusers demanding that his books be burned. Though he appealed to reason, to his conscience, and even to the Word of God, his words went completely unheeded and ignored. He finally fell silent, realizing that nothing he said would be of any use. And even his silence, twisted by his enemies, was spun as an acknowledgment of guilt.

And so, on the morning of July 6, this innocent man of God was marched into the local cathedral to face his final condemnation. His accusers dressed him in priestly robes and put a communion cup in his hand, but only to deride him. Soon they stripped him of these vestments, removing them one by one as a symbolic demonstration of his final excommunication and public shame.

Having been branded as a heretic and denounced by the court, he was paraded to the place of execution—a field outside the city. When he again refused to recant, he was tied to a stake with wet ropes as a chain was secured around his neck. Wood, hay, and kindling were placed at his feet, as the taunts of his executioners intermingled with the hushed voices of the curious crowd. Soon the fire was lit, and smoke began to fill the air. But as the flames sprang up around him, this faithful martyr cried out, not in despair, but with the words of a hymn: "'Christ, thou Son of the living God, have mercy upon us, Christ, thou Son of the living God, have mercy upon me, thou who art born of Mary the Virgin . . .' and when he began to sing the third time, the wind blew the flame into his face and thus praying within himself and moving his lips and head, he expired in the Lord."[1]

But the flames lit on that summer day in 1415 would pale in comparison to the fire of reformation sparked by John Huss's life.[2] His influence had already extended throughout Bohemia and other parts of the Holy Roman Empire. Eventually, it would find its way to an obscure part of Germany, where it would shape the views of a monk named Martin Luther. Upon discovering Huss's writings, Luther exclaimed, "I was overwhelmed with astonishment. I could not understand for what cause they had burnt so great a man who explained the Scriptures with so much gravity and skill."[3] Though separated by a century, Huss would become one of Luther's greatest mentors—to the point that Luther himself would become known as the "Saxon Huss."[4]

But why did the Roman Catholic Church put John Huss to death? If he was a noble scholar and an able teacher of Scripture, what brought about his condemnation and execution?

Huss did not begin his life at odds with the church. In fact, from an early age he desired to become a priest. He was born around 1370 into a poor peasant family in Husinec, Bohemia.[5] Coming from abject

---

1. Matthew Spinka, *John Hus at the Council Constance* (New York: Columbia University Press, 1968), 233. The name "Huss" is sometimes spelled "Hus."

2. For more on the life of John Huss, see Allen W. Schattschneider, *Through Five Hundred Years* (Bethlehem, PA: Comenius Press, 1974); and Oscar Kuhns, *John Huss: The Witness* (New York; Eaton and Mains, 1907).

3. Martin Luther, *Mon. Hus.*, vol. 1, preface, in Herbert Brook Workman and Robert Martin Pope, eds., *The Letters of John Hus* (London: Houder & Stoughton, 1904), 1.

4. Roger Olson, *The Story of Christian Theology* (Downers Grove, IL: InterVarsity Press, 1999), 349.

5. Husinec is in the modern-day Czech Republic. His last name was derived from the town in which he was born. He shortened it to "Huss" (or "Hus"), which meant "Goose" in the Bohemian language. Such became something of a nickname for John Huss, and church history references (by Luther and others) to "the Goose that was cooked" refer to him and his execution.

poverty, Huss pursued the priesthood, in part because his mother encouraged him to do so, but primarily because it guaranteed him a decent living. He would eventually be ordained in 1402.

As a young man, he attended the University of Prague, where he earned several degrees: a bachelor of arts (in 1393), a bachelor of theology (in 1394), and a master of theology (in 1396). In 1398, he began teaching at the university. His rapid success was such that by 1401 he became the dean of the philosophical faculty and by 1402, the rector of the whole university. It was during this time that Huss was greatly influenced by the writings of John Wycliffe—the great English Reformer of a previous generation. Wycliffe's views, especially regarding the authority of Scripture and the corruption of the papacy, would leave an indelible mark on the bright young Huss.

Shortly after his ordination (and in addition to his academic teaching responsibilities), Huss became the preacher of Bethlehem Chapel—the main church in Prague and a facility that could hold up to three thousand people.[6] He preached in the Bohemian language rather than in Latin, a practice that set him apart and made him extremely popular with the people, and unpopular with the clergy.

Teaching through the Scriptures had a dramatic impact on his life, such that he began to recognize the bankruptcy of the Roman Catholic system. Regarding his spiritual transformation he wrote, "When I was young in years and reason, I too belonged to the foolish sect [of Roman Catholicism]. But when the Lord gave me knowledge of scripture, I discharged that kind of stupidity from my foolish mind."[7] It was this

---

6. The chapel was purposely named "Bethlehem" or "House of Bread" because it was a place where the common person could be readily fed from the Word of God.

7. Matthew Spinka, *John Hus' Concept of the Church* (Princeton, NJ: Princeton University Press, 1966), 10.

commitment to the Bible that would come to mark his ministry. In another place he stated, "I humbly accord faith, i.e. trust, to the holy Scriptures, desiring to hold, believe, and assert whatever is contained in them as long as I have breath in me."[8]

When the Roman Catholic Church authorized the sale of indulgences in Prague, Huss publicly denounced the practice—ultimately leading to his excommunication. But even after being censured by the pope, he kept preaching in Bethlehem Chapel. The more he preached, the more heavily he leaned on the Bible, which he unequivocally proclaimed to be the final authority. As one historian explains:

> It is no wonder that Bethlehem chapel was thronged. Its pulpit dealt in no theological abstractions. The sword of the Spirit, which is the Word of God, was in the preacher's hand a sharp weapon, wielded dexterously to lay open the sins and subterfuges of the conscience. It was the Word of Life offering the comforts of saving grace. Huss was a preacher to the age in which he lived, to the congregations which pressed to hear him. His messages burn with zeal for pure religion and with sympathy for men. With his whole heart he was a preacher. Christ's chief command, as he reminded the archbishop of Prague, was to preach the Gospel to every creature, and when he was forbidden by archbishop and pope to longer occupy his pulpit he solemnly declared, in a letter to the chief civil officials of Bohemia, that he dared not obey the commands, for to do so would be to offend "against God and his own salvation."[9]

---

8. *550 Years of Jan Hus' Witness* (Geneva: World Alliance of Reformed Churches, 1965), 1–2.

9. David S. Schaff, *John Huss: His Life, Teachings and Death after Five Hundred Years* (Eugene, OR: Wipf and Stock Publishers, 1915), 41.

In order to make him stop, the ecclesiastical authorities passed an edict that no citizen could receive communion or be buried on church grounds as long as Huss kept preaching. So, in order to spare the people that loss, he finally relented. In 1412 he retired to the country-side, where he studied and wrote feverishly.

Huss's major work, *De Ecclesia* (*The Church*), outlined his major disagreements with the Roman Catholic system of his day. It was read publicly in Prague in 1413, and it contained radical views. For instance, Huss taught that the church was made up of all the predes-tined believers of all ages. This contrasted with the official position of the Roman Catholic Church, which taught that "the pope is the head and the cardinals the body of the Church."[10] Common lay-people were not real members but only communed with the true church through the Lord's Table (which for them was limited only to the bread).

In *De Ecclesia*, Huss also said that the authority of the Bible is greater than the authority of the church. This was an equally radical idea in that day, and it was an idea to which Huss had been intro-duced by John Wycliffe. A hundred years later, Martin Luther would echo this very same conviction.

But the primary reason John Huss was put to death is this: he taught that Jesus Christ alone is the head of the church. Huss denounced the corrupt priests, cardinals, and popes of his day as disqualified from any type of spiritual leadership—arguing instead that the true authority belongs to Christ and His Word. Thus he exclaimed, "If the papal utterances agree with the law of Christ, they are to be obeyed. If they are at variance with it, then Christ's disciples

---

10. Spinka, *John Hus' Concept of the Church*, 261.

must stand loyally and manfully with Christ against all papal bulls whatsoever and be ready, if necessary, to endure malediction and death. When the pope uses his power in an unscriptural way, to resist him is not a sin, it is a mandate."[11] Summarizing Huss's teaching, historian Matthew Spinka wrote:

> In a sermon dealing with Peter, Hus asserts that the Church is not founded on him [Peter] but on "the surest foundation, that is, Christ Jesus." In support of his assertion he quotes Paul's passage, "No other foundation can be laid than that which is laid, which is Christ Jesus." . . . The pope, who has usurped this power, does not wish to hear that Christ asked Peter three times before He granted him the keys whether he loved Him. Only after Peter declared his love for Christ did He bid him to "feed His sheep." Now the pope and many priests do not love God and do not feed the sheep; they do, however, snatch the keys in order to possess worldly power.[12]

Such "statements struck at the root of church authority,"[13] and in response, Rome burned him at the stake.

Not surprisingly, the prominent feature of *De Ecclesia* is "the theme of Christ as the only head of the Church. No one, a mere man, can occupy that position in the same sense. . . . No apostle ever claimed to be the head of the Church, but only a servant of the head, Jesus Christ."[14] Speaking of the reprobate Roman Catholic leadership,

---

11. Ibid., 121.

12. Ibid., 63.

13. Schaff, *John Huss*, 225.

14. Spinka, *John Hus' Concept of the Church*, 259.

Huss exclaimed, "Let the disciples of Antichrist blush who, living contrary to Christ, speak of themselves as the greatest and the proudest of God's holy Church. They, polluted by avarice and arrogance of the world, are called publicly the heads and body of the holy Church. According to Christ's gospel, however, they are called the least."[15] At the end of *De Ecclesia*, as he brought his major work to its conclusion, John Huss closed by thanking God that the true church is not dependent on the pope for its life, because Jesus Christ is its true Lord and Master.[16]

The Catholic Church killed John Huss because he defied papal authority—and he did this by teaching that Jesus Christ alone is the head of the church. Though the pope and cardinals claimed that status for themselves, Huss remained unconvinced and undeterred. And through his preaching, he exposed them as usurpers. As one historian observes, "Huss's career inaugurated the movement of . . . revolt from the absolute authority of the pope and the Roman Catholic church."[17] Huss's commitment to the sovereign lordship of Christ and the supremacy of His Word cost him his life. Yet God used his stand to impact church history forever.

Jesus Christ: The Lord of His Church

The Protestant Reformers who followed after John Huss shared his commitment to the lordship of Christ. This is perhaps seen most

---

15. Ibid., 261, citing *De Ecclesia*, 33.

16. Ibid., 289.

17. Schaff, *John Huss*, 302–3.

clearly in the Reformation principles of *solus Christus* ("Christ alone") and *sola Scriptura* ("Scripture alone"). The Reformers insisted that Jesus Christ, not the pope, is the head of the church. Accordingly, the Word of Christ, and not the magisterium, is the final authority for faith and practice.

This conviction was Martin Luther's main motivation for breaking fellowship with Rome. In his *Table Talk* Luther explained:

> The chief cause that I fell out with the pope was this: the pope boasted that he was the head of the church, and condemned all that would not be under his power and authority. . . . Further he took upon him power, rule, and authority over the Christian church, and over the Holy Scriptures, the Word of God; [claiming that] no man must presume to expound the Scriptures, but only he, and according to his ridiculous conceits; so that he made himself lord over the church.[18]

The arrogance inherent in the papal system[19] was such that Luther remarked, "I am persuaded that if at this time, St. Peter, in person, should preach all the articles of Holy Scripture, and only deny the pope's authority, power, and primacy, and say, that the pope is not the head of all Christendom, they would cause him to be hanged. Yea, if Christ

---

18. Martin Luther, *The Table Talk of Martin Luther*, ed. and trans. William Hazlitt (London: Bell & Daldy, 1872), 203–4.

19. It should be noted that Roman Catholicism still teaches the infallible authority of the pope over the church. Catholic theologian Ludwig Ott, in his *Fundamentals of Catholic Dogma* (Charlotte, NC: Tan Books, 1974), explains the Catholic view: "As the supreme judge of the Church, the Pope has the right of bringing every Church law-matter before his court, and to receive appeals in all Church disputes. He himself is judged by nobody (CIC 1556; *Prima sedes a nemine judicatur*), because there is no higher judge on earth than he. For the same reason there is no appeal to a higher court against the judgment of the Pope" (286).

himself were again on earth, and should preach, without all doubt the pope would crucify him again."[20]

John Calvin raised similar objections, observing that the priests were more concerned with upholding the pope's authority than with honoring Christ or His Word. They did not care "if the glory of God happens to be violated with open blasphemies, provided no one lift a finger against the primacy of the Apostolic See [the pope], and the authority of their holy Mother Church."[21] By contrast, Calvin affirmed "Christ the head of the Church,"[22] contending that "the constitution of the body [the church] will be in a right state, if simply the Head, which furnishes the several members with everything that they have, is allowed, without any hindrance, to have the pre-eminence."[23] After all, "It is the will of God to govern and defend his Church through the mediation of his Son. This is the explanation given by Paul to the Ephesians, that he was set at the right hand of the Father, to be the head over all things to the Church, which is his body.' . . . For the same reason the Scripture often styles him Lord, because the Father has given Him authority over us."[24] No pope or church council can take that authority away from Christ: "Since He is the head of the church, all those who have ever been ordained to rule over the church are subject to Him."[25]

With the names of Huss, Luther, and Calvin, we could list many

---

20. Luther, *Table Talk*, 234.

21. John Calvin, *Institutes of the Christian Religion*, 2 vols., trans. John Allen (Philadelphia: Presbyterian Board of Education, 1921), 1:25.

22. Ibid., 1:155.

23. John Calvin, *Calvin's Commentaries*, 22 vols. (Grand Rapids: Baker, n.d.), 21:198. Calvin was commenting on Colossians 2:19.

24. Calvin, *Institutes of the Christian Religion*, 1:451–52.

25. John Calvin, *Calvin: Commentaries*, ed. Joseph Haroutunian (Louisville: Westminster John Knox Press, 1958), 362. Calvin was commenting on John 12:12–15.

others—Christian leaders like the Protestant Reformer John Knox, the Scottish Puritan Samuel Rutherford, and the American theologian Jonathan Edwards. These faithful believers refused to acknowledge anyone other than Jesus Christ as Lord of the church—whether the would-be usurper was a pope or a king.[26] Summarizing the Protestant perspective in his own inimitable way, renowned preacher Charles Spurgeon declared:

> Of all the dreams that ever deluded men and probably of all blasphemies that ever were uttered, there has never been one which is more absurd and which is more fruitful in all manner of mischief than the idea that the Bishop of Rome can be the head of the church of Jesus Christ. No, these popes die and how could the church live if its head were dead? The true Head ever lives and the church ever liveth in him.[27]

In a sermon entitled "Jesus Our Lord," Spurgeon made the issue crystal clear:

---

26. For example, the English crown attempted to exert absolute control over the church in Scotland during the seventeenth century. For more on the history of these events, see William G. Blaikie, *The Preachers of Scotland* (Edinburgh: T & T Clark, 1888). On page 97, Blaikie explains: "The attempt by the State party to force a new liturgy on the Church, the use of which should be binding under the highest penalties, showed a determination to set aside Christ's authority, and tyrannise over His heritage even in the most sacred region of worship. By the force of reaction the Church was thrown upon the more full assertion of Christ's claims as Head of the Church, and the glorious privilege of the Church to follow her divine Head."

27. Charles Spurgeon, "The Head of the Church," sermon no. 839, *Metropolitan Tabernacle Pulpit* (Pasadena, TX: Pilgrim Publications, 1982), 14:621. Elsewhere, Spurgeon noted that "Christ did not redeem his church with his blood that the Pope might come in and steal away the glory. He never came from heaven to earth, and poured out his very heart that he might purchase his people that a poor sinner, a mere man, should be set upon high to be admired by all the nations, and to call himself God's representative on earth. Christ has always been the head of the church" (Charles Spurgeon, "Christ Glorified," *Metropolitan Tabernacle Pulpit*, 60:592).

The Church of God, in a very special manner, calls Jesus "our Lord," for *there is not, and there cannot be any head of the Church except the Lord Jesus Christ*. It is awful blasphemy for any man on earth to call himself Christ's vicar and the head of the church, and it is a usurpation of the crown rights of King Jesus for any king or queen to be called the head of the church, for the true Church of Jesus Christ can have no head but Jesus Christ himself. I am thankful that there is no head to the church of which I am a member save Jesus Christ himself, nor dare I be a member of any church which would consent to any headship but his.[28]

Like Charles Spurgeon, the faithful throughout church history have always preserved by the Holy Spirit a wholehearted devotion to the true head, Jesus Christ. He alone is the Lord of His church, and that position cannot be occupied by another. John Huss and the Reformers who came after him understood this, which is why they broke away from the corrupt Roman Catholic system. The historical result was the Protestant Reformation.

But what are the practical implications of Christ's lordship for us as believers in the church today? And how does His headship tie in to the slave/master paradigm presented in the New Testament? We will consider those questions in the next two chapters. As we do, we will discover just how central this truth is, not only to our understanding of the corporate church but also to our very identity as individual Christians.

---

28. Charles Spurgeon, "Jesus Our Lord," sermon no. 2806, *Metropolitan Tabernacle Pulpit* (Pasadena, TX: Pilgrim Publications, 1977), 48:558. Emphasis in original.

five

The Lord and Master (Part 2)

T he heroes of church history defended Christ's headship, not on the basis of an arbitrary opinion or out of personal ambition, but because they found that truth unmistakably revealed in the Scriptures. Ephesians 5:23 states that "Christ . . . is the head of the church," and Colossians 1:18 echoes, "He is also head of the body, the church; and He is the beginning, the firstborn from the dead, so that He Himself will come to have first place in everything." In the first chapter of Ephesians, Paul explained that God the Father "put all things in subjection under His [Christ's] feet, and gave Him as head over all things to the church, which is His body, the fullness of Him who fills all in all" (vv. 22–23). Other New Testament Scriptures speak of growing "up in all aspects into Him who is the head" (Eph. 4:15) and "holding fast to the head, from whom the entire body . . . grows with a growth which is from God" (Col. 2:19).

But what does the New Testament mean when it speaks of Christ as the "head of the church"? The Greek word for "head" (*kephalē*) designates "first or superior rank"[1] or "anything *supreme, chief,* [or] *prominent.*"[2] Its

1. Timothy Friberg, Barbara Friberg, and Neva F. Miller, *Analytical Lexicon of the Greek New Testament* (Grand Rapids: Baker Books, 2000), 229. For a detailed discussion of the meaning of *kephalē*, especially as it relates to recent debates in evangelical scholarship, see Wayne Grudem, "The Meaning of κεφαλή ('Head'): An Evaluation of New Evidence, Real and Alleged," *Journal of the Evangelical Theological Society* 44/1 (March 2001), 25–65.

2. Carl Ludwig Wilibald Grimm, *Greek-English Lexicon of the New Testament*, trans. Joseph Henry Thayer (Grand Rapids: Zondervan, 1970), 345.

meaning overlaps with the word *kyrios* ("Lord")[3] and "points to Christ's superior rank or status."[4] To say that Christ is the head of the church is to say that He is the Lord and Master over the church.

In Roman times the "head of the household" possessed "near total powers over members of the household, especially his offspring (including adult offspring) and slaves."[5] As those who are part of the "household of faith" and "the household of God,"[6] our allegiance belongs to our Master, the "head of the household" (cf. Matt. 10:24–25)—namely, the One to whom "all authority has been given . . . in heaven and on earth" (Matt. 28:18).

The New Testament indicates that the Father gave this supreme authority to His Son, having "raised Him from the dead and seated Him at His right hand in the heavenly places, far above all rule and authority and power and dominion, and every name that is named, not only in this age but also in the one to come" (Eph. 1:20–21).[7] After Christ's humiliation and death, "God highly exalted Him, and bestowed on Him the name which is above every name, that at the name of Jesus EVERY KNEE SHOULD BOW, of those who are in heaven,

---

3. Ibid. Grimm notes that "of persons" *kephalē* means "*master, lord.*" Along these same lines, Douglas J. Moo, in *Colossians, Pillar New Testament Commentary* (Grand Rapids: Eerdmans, 2008), commenting on Colossians 1:18, notes that "the basic conception [of *kephalē*] is again a rather straightforward elaboration of the metaphor, based on the standard Christian conception of Christ as the Lord of his people. In the ancient world, the head was conceived to be the governing member of the body, that which both controlled it and provided for its life and sustenance" (128).

4. William W. Klein, *Ephesians, Expositor's Bible Commentary*, rev. ed. (Grand Rapids: Zondervan, 2006), 61.

5. Jennifer A. Glancy, *Slavery in Early Christianity* (Minneapolis: Fortress Press, 2006), 47. Here the author is discussing the Latin term *paterfamilias*, which is rendered as "'father of the family,' or more generally, 'head of the household.'"

6. Gal. 6:10; Eph. 2:19; 1 Tim. 3:15; 1 Peter 4:17.

7. Cf. Matt. 11:27; John 3:35; 17:2; Acts 2:36.

and on earth, and under the earth, and that every tongue will confess that Jesus Christ is Lord, to the glory of God the Father" (Phil. 2:9–11). He is the King of kings and the Lord of lords; His exaltation will be eternal and His authority forever and ever.[8] As the prophet Daniel explained, "To Him was given dominion, glory and a kingdom, that all the peoples, nations and men of every language might serve Him. His dominion is an everlasting dominion which will not pass away; and His kingdom is one which will not be destroyed" (Dan. 7:14).

The overwhelming testimony of Scripture is that Jesus Christ is "Lord of all" (Rom. 10:12) and the "head over all things" (Eph. 1:22), including His body, the church.[9] Accordingly, the true church is made up of those "who in every place call on the name of our Lord Jesus Christ" (1 Cor. 1:2). Whereas false teachers reject His lordship, at least in practice, faithful ministers gladly submit themselves to the authority of Christ and His Word—seeing themselves as slaves in the work of the Chief Shepherd.[10]

Amazingly, in spite of the clear teaching of Scripture and the faithful witness of Protestant church history, most of the trends in contemporary evangelicalism actually attack the lordship of Christ over His church. Some of these attacks are blatant and theological, like the no-lordship position of the so-called Free Grace Movement.

---

8. Rev. 5:12–13; 17:14; 19:16.

9. New Testament references to the church as Christ's body (*soma*) may include a sense of our subservience to Him as His slaves. Murray Harris, in *Slave of Christ* (Downers Grove, IL: InterVarsity Press, 1999), explains: "The word *soma* ('body') ranges in meaning in Greek literature from 'corpse' to 'person', with an emphasis on physicality. But as early as the third century BC, this word, without any qualifying adjective, was used to describe a slave (see LSJ, 1749), who was seen as basically a 'body', possessed by his master for his use. Aristotle (*Pol.* 125. 4a. 16) went one stage further: 'The slave is part of the master, in the sense of being a living but separate part of his body'" (111–12).

10. E.g., 2 Tim. 2:24; 1 Peter 5:3–4.

That movement was especially popular several years ago, which is why I wrote *The Gospel According to Jesus* (in 1988) and *The Gospel According to the Apostles* (in 1993). The Free Grace view twists the gospel message, claiming that neither repentance from sin nor submission to Christ has any part in saving faith. By promoting a form of "easy believism," Free Grace advocates openly deny the sinner's need to repent of sin and to confess Jesus as Lord and Master in the biblical sense of total submission. In so doing, they teach a different gospel altogether, which is "really not another" but an obvious attempt "to distort the gospel of Christ" (Gal. 1:7).

Today, however, the threats are much more subtle, primarily because the contemporary evangelical movement has lost its interest in doctrine. The current of mainstream evangelicalism is driven by pragmatic concerns, not theological ones. Church growth gurus worry about what draws a crowd, not about what the Bible says. Because it successfully appeals to unredeemed flesh, prosperity preachers make *man* the master, as if Christ were some sort of genie in a bottle—obliged to grant health, wealth, and happiness to those who send enough money. Even within some conservative circles, pragmatic worldly methods (including crass humor and coarse speech) and almost boundless adaptations of the worst of worldly music are aggressively defended as long as they get visible results. The sad reality is that popularity, not faithfulness to Christ and His Word, has become evangelicalism's new standard of measure and its current brand of no-lordship ideology.

As a result, the Scriptures have been systematically replaced with whatever else is deemed more relevant or entertaining. The entrepreneurialism of the independent church movement has made it popular for a thousand would-be "christs" to build their own media empires, labeling themselves *pastors* and their organizations *churches*. But these ministry moguls are not interested in building the true church, a fact evidenced by their indifference to propositional truth and their eagerness to gain mass appeal by minimizing both the Word of God and the lordship of Christ. They water down the gospel, shorten their already shallow sermons, and adapt a market-driven strategy for ministry. In so doing, they rebel against Christ!

The Lord expresses His rule in His church insofar as the Scripture is preached, explained, applied, and obeyed. To diminish the dominating role of Scripture in the life of the church is to treat the Lord of the church as if His revelation were optional. It is nothing short of mutiny. And the seriousness of such revolt cannot be comprehended. Nonbiblical ministry, non-expository preaching, and non-doctrinal teaching usurp Christ's headship, silencing His voice to His sheep. That kind of devastating approach steals the mind of Christ away from the body of Christ, builds indifference toward His Word, and quenches the work of His Spirit. It removes protection from error and sin, eliminates transcendence and clarity, cripples worship, and sows seeds of compromise. It deflects the honor due to the true head of the church, and the Lord does not take kindly to those who would steal His glory.[11]

Personal Savior, Personal Lord

The undeniable assertion of Scripture is that Jesus Christ is the Lord of His church—even if many within mainstream evangelicalism fail to reflect that reality in their activities. But the lordship of Christ is not

11. See Isaiah 42:8; 48:11; Ezekiel 34:8–10; Acts 12:23.

merely a corporate concept. It is also highly personal. In the same way that Christ is Lord of His church collectively, He is also the Lord and Master of each believer individually. When we affirm His headship over the whole church, we simultaneously and necessarily acknowledge His lordship over ourselves and every other member of His body.[12]

In Roman times, it was not uncommon for dozens, or even hundreds, of slaves to serve the same master.[13] As members of his extended household, they were accountable to the one master both as a group and as individuals. The same is true of the church, where Christ is the head not merely of the corporate body but also of each individual believer. He is both the Savior and the Lord for each person who calls on Him (Acts 2:21).

When we call Jesus "Lord," we are clearly acknowledging Him as sole Master. The Greek word for "Lord" is *kyrios,* and it occurs nearly 750 times in the New Testament. Its fundamental meaning is "master,"

---

12. Referring to the Scottish reformation of the seventeenth century, William G. Blaikie noted the integral relationship of these two doctrines, though from the reverse perspective: "The men of those times did not, like so many now, deem it enough to recognize Christ's headship over themselves personally; they joined to that with all the ardour of their nature, His headship over the whole Church. To repudiate the one was as great a crime and as great a folly as to repudiate the other. To deny His place as King in Zion was to imperil their personal relation to Him almost as much as to deny His atonement or His mediation" (*The Preachers of Scotland* [Edinburgh: T & T Clark, 1888], 98).

13. William Smith and A. S. Wilkins, *A Dictionary of Greek and Roman Antiquities* (London: John Murray, 1891), s.v. "Servus," 664. The authors explain that "under the [Roman] Empire the number of domestic slaves greatly increased, and in every family of importance there were separate slaves to attend to all the necessities of domestic life. It was considered a reproach to a man not to keep a considerable number of slaves. . . . Horace (*Sat.* i. 3, 12) seems to speak of ten slaves as the lowest number which a person in tolerable circumstances ought to keep . . . [while] a freedman under Augustus, who had lost much property in the Civil Wars, left at his death as many as 4,116 (Plin. *H. N.* xxxiii. § 135). Two hundred was no uncommon number for one person to keep (Hor. *Sat.* i. 3, 11), and Augustus permitted even a person that was exiled to take twenty slaves or freedmen with him (Dio Cass. lvi. 27)" (656–67).

or "owner," making it the relational counterpart to the word *slave* (*doulos*).[14] As Murray Harris explains:

> When believers sing or recite the confession "Jesus is Lord," we are affirming his absolute supremacy, not only over the physical and moral universe (Matt. 28:18; 1 Pet. 3:22), and not only over human history (Rom. 9:5), not only over all human beings (Acts 10:36; Rom. 10:12), whether living or dead (Rom. 14:9), not only over the church (Eph. 1:22), but also over our own lives as his willing slaves. The simple but crucial point is that the two words "Lord" and "slave," kyrios and doulos, are correlatives.[15]

Kyrios and *doulos* are two sides of the same relationship. To be a *doulos* was to have a master. And vice versa, a *kyrios* by definition was the owner of slaves. Thus, to confess Jesus as "Lord" is to simultaneously confess Him as Master and ourselves as His slaves.

In New Testament times, the *kyrios* had full authority over the life of his slaves[16]—whether those slaves worked out in the fields or in the

---

14. In social settings, the term could also serve as a respectful greeting (similar to "Sir"), indicating the superiority or supremacy of the one being addressed. Its primary social connection, however, was to the word *doulos* ("slave"). By definition, the *kyrios* is "the possessor and disposer of a thing [or person]; the owner; one who has control of the person, the master" (*Strong's Enhanced Lexicon*, entry 2962). From a theological perspective, this master/slave connection is unmistakable when *kyrios* is used in reference to deity. Thus, Werner Foerster explains that "κύριος, then, is particularly used in expression of a personal relationship of man to the deity, whether in prayer, thanksgiving or vow, and as a correlate of δοῦλος inasmuch as the man concerned describes as κύριος the god under whose orders he stands" (*Theological Dictionary of the New Testament*, unabridged, ed. Gerhard Kittel, trans. Geoffrey W. Bromiley [Grand Rapids: Eerdmans, 1965], s.v. "κύριος," 3:1052). Likewise, Gottfried Quell notes that "in the religious sphere, *kyrios* is reserved for God" (*Theological Dictionary of the New Testament* [abridged], s.v. "κύριος," 488).

15. Harris, *Slave of Christ*, 90.

16. Cf. Matt. 8:9; 13:27–28; 18:31–34; 21:34–36; 24:45–51; 25:23, 26–30; Mark 13:34–35; Luke 12:37; 14:16–24; 17:7–10.

master's house. He could give his slaves any task, like sending them on an errand or entrusting them with his estate during his absence. If they performed well, he could reward them, or simply do nothing since they had done only what was expected. If they failed, the master could punish them accordingly, perhaps by inflicting a severe beating, or even selling them if he so desired. The complete supremacy of the master over the slave was so culturally ingrained that Jesus could even use it as a truism in His teachings—noting that no slave was greater than his *kyrios*.[17]

Significantly, the term *kyrios* not only overlapped with the Greek word *kephalē* ("head"), but was also synonymous with the word *despotes*,[18] from which we derive the English word *despot*. The New Testament uses *despotes* to refer to both human masters and the divine Master.[19] The term itself "originally referred to an 'owner' or 'possessor' of persons or things within a household—a sense made explicit by the compound word *oiko-despotes*, 'the master of the house.' When the term is applied to God or to Jesus, it emphasizes absoluteness of ownership, or authority, and of power."[20]

Understanding the meaning of *kyrios* and its synonyms is critical because it underscores for us what it means to be a slave of Christ. Modern readers, removed by two millennia from the social milieu of the ancient Roman Empire, can easily skip past terms like "lord," "master," and "slave" without fully appreciating the truth conveyed by the terms.[21]

---

17. Matt. 10:24; cf. John 13:16; 15:15, 20.

18. According to Werner Foerster, "In the *koine* δεσπότης [*despotes*] and κύριος [*kyrios*] are to a large degree used alongside one another. The κύριος is the owner of slaves and property" (*Theological Dictionary of the New Testament*, unabridged, s.v. "κύριος," 3:1043).

19. 1 Tim. 6:1–2; 2 Tim. 2:21; 2 Peter 2:1; cf. Luke 2:29.

20. Harris, *Slave of Christ*, 111–12.

21. Francis Lyall has noted that "the relationship of a slave to his owner, and of a freed slave to his former owner (his patron), had aspects and overtones, that are not present to our minds

But for those living in a first-century context, there was no mistaking what it meant to call oneself a slave and to call another *Lord* and *Master*.

When Paul told his readers that they were "bought with a price" (1 Cor. 7:23), and that though they were once "slaves of sin" they are now "slaves of righteousness" (Rom. 6:17–18), they knew exactly what he meant. Paul's declaration in Romans 14 certainly underscores the point: "For not one of us lives for himself, and not one dies for himself; for if we live, we live for the Lord, or if we die, we die for the Lord; therefore whether we live or die, we are the Lord's" (vv. 7–8). Commenting on these verses, Murray Harris observed:

> Notable is the threefold repetition of *kyrios* in verse 8: the Master is the focal point of the slave's life; everything is evaluated in terms of the Master's pleasure and profit. The absoluteness is depicted in temporal terms—the Master's good reigns supreme, whether in continuation of his slave's life or with the advent of his slave's death. Believers are divine property, invested at the discretionary will of the Master for his own profit.[22]

The slave was completely subservient to the master, living in "a state of absolute subjection. . . . His very identity is imposed by the owner who gives him his name."[23]

---

today. For us, the concept of the slave has been attenuated by nonexistence in our day-to-day world. Most think rather romantically of slavery as they read about it in the Epistles. There is a certain quaint charm in being 'a slave of Christ' because we are accustomed to speak of ourselves as 'slaves' only metaphorically. The reality was rather different" (*Slaves, Citizens, Sons: Legal Metaphors in the Epistles* [Grand Rapids: Academie Books, 1984], 28).

22. Harris, *Slave of Christ*, 112. Regarding this passage, he notes: "Nowhere in the New Testament is the absoluteness of the Lord's ownership of his *douloi* [slaves] depicted more clearly than in Romans 14:7–8."

23. Thomas Wiedemann, *Greek and Roman Slavery* (New York: Routledge, 1988), 1.

To "confess with your mouth Jesus as Lord" (Rom. 10:9) is to simultaneously acknowledge one's own obligation to obey Him with total submission. His will is absolutely sovereign, and His slaves are expected to obey no matter the level of sacrifice required. In that context, Christ's words in Luke 9:23 take on the full weight of their meaning: "If anyone wishes to come after Me, he must deny himself, and take up his cross daily and follow Me." To follow the Master is to come to the end of oneself and submit completely to His will. Anyone who would be His disciple must also be His slave. Those unwilling to give up everything to follow Him are not worthy of Him. As the Lord Himself said, "He who loves father or mother more than Me is not worthy of Me; and he who loves son or daughter more than Me is not worthy of Me. And he who does not take his cross and follow after Me is not worthy of Me. He who has found his life will lose it, and he who has lost his life for My sake will find it" (Matt. 10:37–39).

When the New Testament writers referred to themselves as "slaves of Christ," they underscored their total submission to the lordship of Jesus Christ. For the apostle Paul, this involved nothing less than a life of daily self-sacrifice, wholly lived for the sake of his Master. As one scholar explains:

> [S]ince the slave was not legally a person, he could own no property and he did not even have power over himself. He only did what he was told to do. This in measure indicates the extent of Paul's self-surrender to his Master. . . . [F]or Paul, "the slave of Christ," all his goods, time, ambitions, and purposes were subject to the determination of Christ. Paul was no different from the ordinary slave: he was at his Master's disposal. He was also *only* at his Master's disposal. Just as a man can serve only one master (Matt. 6:24; Luke 16:13), so he

was responsible only to his Master (Rom. 14:4), a liberating thought for those dogged by the opinions of others.[24]

Hence, Paul could ask the Roman believers, "Who are you to judge the servant of another? To his own master he stands or falls; and he will stand, for the Lord is able to make him stand" (Rom. 14:4). He could tell the Philippians that "to live is Christ" (Phil. 1:21) and that "whatever things were gain to me, those things I have counted as loss for the sake of Christ" (Phil. 3:7). To the Galatians, Paul could exclaim, "It is no longer I who live, but Christ lives in me" (Gal. 2:20); and to the Corinthians he could declare that those transformed by the gospel "no longer live for themselves, but for Him who died and rose again on their behalf" (2 Cor. 5:15). Elsewhere, he exhorted his readers with these words: "Do you not know . . . that you are not your own? For you have been bought with a price: therefore glorify God in your body" (1 Cor. 6:19–20).

To the Colossians, Paul would similarly underscore the all-encompassing implications of Christ's sovereign lordship: "Whatever you do in word or deed, do all in the name of the Lord Jesus" (Col. 3:17), even telling the slaves in that congregation, "Whatever you do, do your work heartily, as for the Lord" (v. 23). Over and over again, perhaps more than any other theme, Paul's writings evidence an intimate understanding of the subservient relationship of a believer to Christ—namely, that Jesus is his Master and he is but a slave.

---

24. Lyall, *Slaves, Citizens, Sons,* 37–38.

six

Our Lord and Our God

Paul's perspective on the lordship of Christ was certainly not unique to him. As we saw in chapter 2, the New Testament writers repeatedly spoke of themselves and their fellow believers as slaves of Christ. From the moment they made the saving confession "Jesus is Lord," there was no question that He was their Master—such that they were bound to submit to Him in everything.

But the apostles understood that Jesus Christ, being God in human flesh, is far more than any earthly *kyrios*. He is the Lord over every other lord, and the King over every other king.[1] Put succinctly, He is the "Lord of all" (Acts 10:36), possessing the full weight of divine authority, for "in Him all the fullness of Deity dwells in bodily form . . . and He is the head over all rule and authority" (Col. 2:9–10). He has been seated at "the right hand of the power of God" (Luke 22:69 NKJV), and all things have been put "in subjection under His feet" (Eph. 1:22). Of Him, the author of Hebrews wrote, "He is the radiance of His [Father's] glory and the exact representation of His nature, and upholds all things by the word of His power. When He had made purification of sins, He sat down at the right hand of the Majesty on high" (1:3). Jesus Christ is "our great God and Savior" (Titus 2:13), the divine Word made flesh,[2] and the promised Messiah, of whom it was

---

1. Cf. Rev. 17:14; 19:16.

2. John 1:1; cf. 5:18.

foretold, "His name will be called Wonderful Counselor, Mighty God, Eternal Father, Prince of Peace" (Isa. 9:6). The man born blind was not wrong to worship Him after proclaiming, "Lord, I believe" (John 9:38). Neither was Thomas wrong to address Him as "my Lord and my God!" (John 20:28). He is the great I AM,[3] and His throne "is forever and ever" (Heb. 1:8 NKJV), for "His kingdom will have no end" (Luke 1:33). Consequently, when the New Testament writers referred to Christ as *kyrios*, they were not only underscoring His authority as Master, they were also affirming His glorious character as God.

By the time the New Testament was written, the name *kyrios* ("Lord") was already a well-known title for God. The Septuagint (the Greek translation of the Old Testament used in Jesus' day) used *kyrios* to translate two different Hebrew names for God—*Adonai* and *Yahweh*. The title *Adonai* (from the root *adon*) literally means "master" and corresponds to the Hebrew word for slave (*'ebed*). It "denotes His sovereign power"[4] and emphasizes the relationship between God as the Master and His people as His slaves (cf. Mal. 1:6). When *kyrios* is used to translate *Adonai* in the Septuagint, "it stresses the fact that as the Liberator from Egypt, or as the Creator, God has a valid right to control over his people and the universe. He is sovereign in the absolute sense."[5]

---

3. John 8:58 (NKJV); cf. Ex. 3:14; John 17:5, 24.

4. Gottfried Quell, in Gerhard Kittel, ed.; and Geoffrey W. Bromiley, trans., *Theological Dictionary of the New Testament* (unabridged) (Grand Rapids: Eerdmans, 1965), s.v. "κύριος," 3:1060. Quell's contribution is included within Werner Foerster's larger dictionary entry. (See chap. 5, n. 18.)

5. Gottfried Quell, *Theological Dictionary of the New Testament Abridged in One Volume*, Kittel and Gerhard Friedrich, eds.; Geoffrey Bromiley, trans. (Grand Rapids: Eerdmans, 1985), under "Kyrios," 491. Along these same lines, John Byron has observed, "God's designation of the Israelites as 'my people' is a claim of ownership that predates and supersedes any claims by Pharaoh. Pharaoh's refusal to acquiesce represents his rejection of God's authority over him and the people he has enslaved. Egypt suffers with plagues and the king of Egypt remains determined not to release the slaves and instead oppresses them even more (5.3–21). . . . The

But the Septuagint also used *kyrios* to translate *Yahweh*—the covenant name of God. Out of respect for the third commandment (Ex. 20:7), the Jews refused even to speak the name *Yahweh* lest they somehow take it in vain. In their prayers and sermons, they would use *Adonai* in its place. It is likely that the translators of the Septuagint, for this reason, translated *Yahweh* with the same word they used for *Adonai*.[6] But whatever the explanation, the fact remains that *kyrios* is used consistently throughout the Septuagint for both *Adonai* and *Yahweh*.[7]

The New Testament writers relied heavily on the Septuagint, frequently quoting from it when they referenced the Old Testament. As a result, they were well acquainted with the dual function *kyrios* served in reference to God, as a term that meant "Master" (equivalent to *Adonai*) and also as the Greek rendering of the divine name *Yahweh*.[8] It was with this dual function in mind that the apostles gladly applied the title *kyrios* to Jesus Christ—the one whom they acknowledged to be both *Adonai* and *Yahweh*. The term was broad enough to "express the comprehensive lordship of Jesus" such that Old Testament "passages [from the Septuagint] which spoke of the κύριος [*kyrios*] could be referred to Jesus. In Him God acts as is said of the κύριος in the OT."[9]

Exodus event represents the transference of Israel from ownership by the king of Egypt to the king of Heaven, God" (*Slavery Metaphors in Early Judaism and Pauline Christianity* [Tubingen, Germany: J. C. B. Mohr, 2003], 49).

6. Centuries later, in the eighth century AD, the Masorites would similarly apply the vowel pointings from *Adonai* to the divine name *Yahweh*.

7. Quell, *Theological Dictionary of the New Testament* (unabridged), s.v. "κύριος," 3:1058. Quell observes that "the word κύριος [*kyrios*], 'lord,' as a name for God in the LXX [Septuagint] is a strict translation only in cases where it is used for אָדוֹן [*Adon*] or אֲדֹנָי [*Adonai*] (in the *ketib*). As a rule, however, it is used as an expository equivalent for the divine name יהוה [*Yahweh*]."

8. Examples of places where *kyrios* is used for *Adonai* include: Matt. 9:38; 11:25; Acts 17:24; 1 Tim. 6:15; Rev. 4:11. Examples of places where *kyrios* is used for *Yahweh* include: Matt. 4:7; 22:37; Mark 12:11; Heb. 7:21.

9. Foerster, *Theological Dictionary of the New Testament* (unabridged), s.v. "κύριος," 3:1094.

The New Testament writers repeatedly emphasized Christ's divine authority and equality with God by ascribing the name *kyrios* to Him.[10] For the believers of the early church, the title *kyrios* denoted Christ not only as their absolute Master but also as God. When we confess Jesus as *Lord*, we similarly acknowledge our duty to both obey Him as King and worship Him as Deity.

In the same way that Old Testament saints viewed themselves as the slaves of Yahweh, we are to view ourselves as the slaves of Jesus Christ. As one author points out:

> Corresponding to Christ's absolute and exclusive ownership of believers in him is their total and sole devotion to him. Isaiah 44:5 indicates that after the exile some faithful Jews would unashamedly say, "I belong to Yahweh," while others would actually write "Yahweh's" on their hands, to indicate whose slaves they were. Most Christians do not bear any "brand-marks of Jesus" (Gal. 6:17) as Paul did, but they might rightly say, "I belong to Christ" (*cf.* 1 Cor. 1:12), and may, figuratively speaking, write "Christ's" on their hands, to indicate whose slaves they are.[11]

In 1 Corinthians 12:3, the apostle Paul makes an astounding statement: "No one can say, 'Jesus is Lord,' except by the Holy Spirit." Certainly, there are many who give lip service to the lordship of Christ but who have never experienced the Spirit's life-giving work (cf. Matt. 7:21–23). Yet, to genuinely acknowledge Jesus' lordship involves both a willingness to obey Him as Master and an eagerness to worship Him

---

10. E.g., Matt. 7:21; 12:8; 22:44–45; John 1:23; 9:38; Rom. 14:9; Acts 10:36; Phil. 2:10–11; 1 Cor. 2:16; Heb. 1:10.

11. Murray J. Harris, *Slave of Christ* (Downers Grove, IL: InterVarsity Press, 1999), 113.

as God. And that happens only in a heart transformed by the Spirit of God, which is why true conversion always includes the heartfelt confession that Jesus is Lord.[12]

Why Do You Call Me "Lord, Lord"?

As those who confess the lordship of Christ, believers are duty bound to obey Him in everything. Along these lines, the *Theological Dictionary of the New Testament* explains: "With his work of redemption Christ has made believers his own possession and now gives them the goals that shape their lives. This new commitment, which is a commitment to righteousness (Rom. 6:19), holiness (1 Thess. 3:13), and newness of life (Rom. 6:4), finds expression in the description of Christians as Christ's *doúloi* [*slaves*] (1 Cor. 7:22; Eph. 6:6)."[13] Slaves of Christ are to be "always abounding in the work of the Lord" (1 Cor. 15:58), "trying to learn what is pleasing to the Lord" (Eph. 5:10), and ever seeking to "understand what the will of the Lord is" (Eph. 5:17).[14] Rightly regarding themselves as "a people for His own possession, zealous for good deeds" (Titus 2:14), they obey the Word of God with eagerness.[15] They understand and embrace the ethical implications of being a slave of

---

12. See Romans 10:9–13; cf. Acts 2:21; 16:30–31. Commenting on 1 Corinthians 12:3, Murray Harris has observed: "What the apostle is saying is that apart from the Holy Spirit's power in enlightening the mind and captivating the will, no person can make this simple confession with understanding and commitment" (*Slave of Christ*, 88–89).

13. Karl Heinrich Rengstorf, in Gerhard Kittel and Gerhard Friedrich, eds.; Geoffrey Bromiley, trans., *Theological Dictionary of the New Testament Abridged in One Volume*, s.v. "doúlos," 185.

14. Cf. 1 Cor. 7:32, 35; 8:6; Col. 1:10; 3:22.

15. Cf. James 1:21–25; 1 Peter 2:9.

Christ, knowing that "the eyes of the Lord are on the righteous, and His ears are open to their prayer, but the face of the Lord is against those who do evil" (1 Peter 3:12 NKJV). As a result, they pursue lives of holiness, longing to be fit for the Master's service.[16]

As Paul explained to Timothy:

> The firm foundation of God stands, having this seal, "The Lord knows those who are His," and, "Everyone who names the name of the Lord is to abstain from wickedness." Now in a large house there are not only gold and silver vessels, but also vessels of wood and of earthenware, and some to honor and some to dishonor. Therefore, if anyone cleanses himself from these things, he will be a vessel for honor, sanctified, useful to the Master, prepared for every good work. Now flee from youthful lusts and pursue righteousness, faith, love and peace, with those who call on the Lord from a pure heart. (2 Tim. 2:19–22)

As slaves to righteousness, believers are "under obligation" (Rom. 8:12; cf. 6:18) to honor God in how they live. Yet, for those who belong to Christ, the motivation to obey is far more profound than mere duty. "If you *love* Me, you will keep My commandments," Jesus told His disciples (John 14:15, emphasis added); and again, "If anyone loves Me, he will keep My Word" (v. 23). The apostle John echoed Christ's words in his epistles: "For this is the love of God, that we keep His commandments; and His commandments are not burdensome" (1 John 5:3); and elsewhere, "This is love, that we walk according to His commandments" (2 John 6). Genuine believers are characterized by a deep love

---

16. Cf. Rom. 12:11; Col. 2:6; 1 Peter 1:16.

for Christ, and that love inevitably manifests itself in obedience.[17] By contrast, those who do not love the Lord, either in what they say or by how they live, evidence the fact that they do not belong to Him.[18]

The only right response to Christ's lordship is wholehearted submission, loving obedience, and passionate worship. Those who give verbal assent to His deity, yet live in patterns of unrepentant disobedience, betray the hypocrisy of their profession. To them, the terrifying weight of Christ's question, "Why do you call Me, 'Lord, Lord,' and do not do what I say?" (Luke 6:46) directly applies. As He warned the crowds at the end of the Sermon on the Mount, after describing the dangers of hypocrisy:

> Not everyone who says to Me, "Lord, Lord," will enter the kingdom of heaven, but he who does the will of My Father who is in heaven will enter. Many will say to Me on that day, "Lord, Lord, did we not prophesy in Your name, and in Your name cast out demons, and in Your name perform many miracles?" And then I will declare to them, "I never knew you; DEPART FROM ME, YOU WHO PRACTICE LAWLESS-NESS" (Matt. 7:21–23).

Clearly, not all who claim to know the Lord actually do. Those who truly "belong to Christ Jesus have crucified the flesh with its passions and desires" (Gal. 5:24). Rather than walking in the flesh, they now "walk by the Spirit" (v. 25), being characterized by a growing desire to obey the Word of God. As Jesus told the crowds in John 8:31, "If you

---

17. 1 Cor. 8:3; Eph. 6:24; 1 Peter 1:8; cf. Mark 12:30; John 21:15–17; 1 John 2:3.

18. 1 Cor. 16:22; cf. John 8:42; Rom. 8:9.

continue in My Word, then you are truly disciples of Mine."[19] After all, "each tree is known by its own fruit" (Luke 6:44); and genuine conversion is always marked by the fruit of repentance and the fruit of the Spirit.[20] Loving obedience is the defining evidence of salvation, such that the two are inseparably linked; as the author of Hebrews explains: "He became to all those who obey Him the source of eternal salvation" (5:9).[21]

The rest of the New Testament issues similar warnings to anyone who might claim to belong to Christ while persisting in unrepentant sin.[22] The first epistle of John is especially clear in this regard. There John wrote, "If we say that we have fellowship with Him and yet walk in the darkness, we lie and do not practice the truth" (1 John 1:6). And later, "Little children, make sure no one deceives you; the one who practices righteousness is righteous, just as He is righteous; the one who practices sin is of the devil. . . . No one who is born of God practices sin. . . . By this the children of God and the children of the devil are obvious: anyone who does not practice righteousness is not of God, nor the one who does not love his brother" (3:7–10). Though many call themselves "Christians," the true condition of anyone's heart is ultimately seen in how he lives. As the saying goes, actions speak louder than words. The profession of faith that never evidences itself in righteous behavior is a "dead" faith (James 2:17), being no better than that of the demons (v. 19). This is not to say that true believers never stumble. Certainly they do. Yet the pattern of their lives is one of

---

19. Cf. John 6:66–69; Matt. 24:13; Col. 1:22–23; 1 Tim. 4:16; Heb. 3:14; 10:38–39; 1 John 2:19.

20. Luke 3:8; Gal. 5:22–23.

21. Cf. John 3:36; Rom. 1:5; 6:16; 15:18; 16:19, 26; 1 Peter 1:2, 22.

22. Rom. 8:9; 1 Cor. 6:9–10; Eph. 5:5–6; Heb. 6:4–8; James 2:17–19.

continual repentance and increasing godliness as they grow in sanctification and Christlikeness.

In the Company of the King

To be a slave of Jesus Christ is the greatest benediction imaginable. Not only is He a kind and gracious Lord, but He is also the God of the universe. His character is perfect; His love is infinite; His power, matchless; His wisdom, unsearchable; and His goodness, beyond compare.[23] It is no wonder, then, that our relationship to Him as our Master brings us great benefit and honor.

In Roman times, one's experience as a slave was almost entirely dependent on the nature of one's master. The slave of a good, benevolent master could expect to be well cared for, enjoying a secure and peaceful life. As one historian explains:

> The material life of the slave in the Roman world, as in later slave societies, was determined [largely] ... by the degree of responsibility with which the master met his (or her) material obligations to the slave. ... In comparison with the free poor, therefore, slaves may often have been at something of a material advantage: given that they were to some degree provided for, they must in many cases have enjoyed a security in their lives that the free poor could never have known.[24]

---

23. John 10:11, 14, 28; Rom. 8:38–39; 11:33–36; 1 Cor. 15:25–26; 1 Peter 1:19; 1 John 3:3.

24. Keith Bradley, *Slavery and Society at Rome* (Cambridge, UK: Cambridge University Press, 1994), 89, 92.

In the same way that wicked owners often made life unbearable for their slaves, a gracious master could make the situation pleasant and even desirable for those in his household.[25] Such a master would evoke the loyalty and love of his slaves, as they served him out of devotion and not just duty. Moreover, "the good owner looked after and cared for his slaves throughout their lives, into retirement. He would not seek to rid himself of the slave that was no longer 'useful' by reason of age or infirmity. That God is a good 'owner' of his 'slaves' is both axiomatic and reassuring."[26]

Because the Lord is our Master, we can trust Him to take care of us in every situation and stage of life. Even in the most difficult of circumstances, He will provide all that we need in order to be faithful to Him.[27] We can be "anxious for nothing" (Phil. 4:6) because we know "that God causes all things to work together for good to those who love God, to those who are called according to His purpose" (Rom. 8:28). We are right to trust Him completely, for He is sovereign not only over our lives, but also over everything that exists.[28] "For He Himself has said, 'I will never leave you nor forsake you.' So we boldly say: 'The Lord is my helper: I will not fear. What can man do to me?'" (Heb. 13:5–6 NKJV).

Such promises have been the bedrock of comfort and hope for every generation of God's people. As David declared in his most famous psalm, "The LORD is my Shepherd, I shall not want. He makes

---

25. Scott Bartchy gives examples from ancient Roman literature of both extreme cruelty and great kindness shown by masters to slaves (*First-Century Slavery* [Eugene, OR: Wipf and Stock Publishers, 2002], 68–69).

26. Francis Lyall, *Slaves, Citizens, Sons: Legal Metaphors in the Epistles* (Grand Rapids: Academic Books, 1984), 38.

27. Cf. Matt. 6:31–33; Phil. 4:19; 2 Cor. 9:8.

28. Cf. Matt. 28:18; Rom. 14:7–9; Eph. 1:20–23; Col. 2:10; James 4:13–15.

me lie down in green pastures; He leads me beside quiet waters. He restores my soul; He guides me in the paths of righteousness for His name's sake. Even though I walk through the valley of the shadow of death, I fear no evil, for You are with me" (23:1–4). A few verses later, he concluded with this resounding expectation, "Surely goodness and lovingkindness will follow me all the days of my life, and I will dwell in the house of the LORD forever" (v. 6). Only a believer can have that kind of certain hope—a calming confidence founded on the bedrock of the Master's gracious character.

To live under the Lord's sovereign protection and care brings immeasurable comfort, joy, and "the peace of God, which surpasses all comprehension" (Phil. 4:7). But the blessings of being His slave go beyond mere *provision*. To be the slave of Christ is also a position of great *privilege*, for we are in the company of none other than the King of the universe. Obviously, we can be associated with no one greater.

Here a parallel can once again be drawn with the slaves of ancient Rome. In New Testament times, slaves derived their own status from the social standing of their masters, such that "slavery to an important person bestowed on the slave a certain amount of prestige and power, a status-by-association."[29] To be the slave of an influential and well-respected master was itself an esteemed position, to the point that slaves would often include the names of their owners on their tombstones. As Dale Martin explains:

> Information about the owners mentioned in [tombstone] inscriptions demonstrates that the slaves were aware that their influence derived from that of their owners. Often a slave mentioned the senatorial or

---

29. Dale B. Martin, *Slavery as Salvation* (New Haven, CT: Yale University Press, 1990), xxii.

consular rank of the owner or gave the master's title (for example, *primipilus*, the senior centurion of a legion). One (probably) slave Pragmateutes in 247–248 C.E. wrote on his family's tombstone that his master was "thrice asiarch." On another tombstone, Agathopous, a slave agent, neglected to give the names of his wife and children (he may not yet have had them), but he was careful to give the Roman name of his master. In each of these cases, the slave noted status symbols of his owner and thereby basked in the reflected light.[30]

Recognizing that their own social standing was derived from their owners' reputations, Roman slaves were glad to associate themselves with their masters—even on their tombstone inscriptions! After all, "naming oneself the slave of an important person was a way of claiming status for oneself. . . . Slaves and freedpersons did not hesitate to call themselves such. They used the term ["slave"] as a title and as an opportunity to link themselves to more powerful people. They seemed to feel no shame in their slavery as long as they could enjoy this status-by-association."[31]

From a secular Roman perspective, there could be no greater master than the emperor, which is why the slaves of Caesar were held in especially high regard. "The slave of a shoemaker likely had little status, but the slave of a local power broker or of a respected aristocrat could in turn hold considerable power and respect. A slave of Caesar was even higher, potentially holding power and enjoying an informal status rivaling important free provincials."[32] To be the personal slave of

---

30. Ibid., 18.

31. Ibid., 47.

32. Ibid., 48.

Caesar was to be in a uniquely influential and respected position: "The unique status of the emperor gave his slaves and freedmen a privileged position—such slaves were allowed to marry citizen-women, and their status was such that people might enroll themselves in this household voluntarily. Evidence from literature and inscriptions throws light on the specialized household and administrative tasks of these slaves and freedmen."[33]

But if it was considered an honor to be the slave of one of the Caesars, it is infinitely more so to be the slave of Christ—the King of kings and Lord of lords! Is it any wonder that the New Testament writers eagerly attributed the title "slave of Christ" to themselves and others? It was not only an affirmation of their complete submission to the Master; it was also a declaration of the privileged position every Christian enjoys by being associated with the Lord. No affiliation could be greater than that.

As slaves, believers have no intrinsic glory in themselves. But as members of the Lord's household, we are distinguished simply by our connection to Him. To be His *doulos* is an incomparable honor.[34] Thus, the apostle Paul can instruct His readers that, if they wish to boast, they should boast only in the Lord.[35]

What a joy and privilege it is to be a slave of the eternal King! Forever we will sing His praises, basking in the radiance of His glory

---

33. Thomas Wiedemann, *Greek and Roman Slavery* (New York: Routledge, 1988), 9.

34. Rengstorf, *Theological Dictionary of the New Testament* (abridged), s.v. "doúlos," 183. Speaking of the Septuagint, the author observes, "[T]he only right thing for the elect people is exclusive service of the Lord (Judg. 10:16; Ps. 2:11, etc.). For this reason *doúloi* is a title of honor when conferred on such outstanding figures as Moses (Josh. 14:7), Joshua (Judg. 2:8) Abraham (Ps. 105:42)[,] David (Ps. 89:3), and Jacob (representing Israel, Is. 48:20). The opposite of *douleúein* is disobedience."

35. 1 Cor. 1:31; 2 Cor. 10:17; Phil. 3:8.

and worshipping Him with hearts full of reverence and love. His name is above any other, and His name will be written on our foreheads for all eternity.[36] Along with the saints of every age, we will never cease to marvel at the fact that, in spite of our own faults and frailties, the Lord chose us to be His own.[37] There is no greater honor than to be in the company of the King.

Therefore, we exult with the psalmist:

> *O come, let us sing for joy to the LORD,*
> *Let us shout joyfully to the rock of our salvation.*
> *Let us come before His presence with thanksgiving,*
> *Let us shout joyfully to Him with psalms.*
> *For the LORD is a great God*
> *And a great King above all gods. . . .*
> *Come, let us worship and bow down,*
> *Let us kneel before the LORD our Maker.*
> *For He is our God,*
> *And we are the people of His pasture and the sheep of His hand.*
> *(95:1–3, 6–7)*

---

36. Phil. 2:9–11; Rev. 22:4

37. Cf. Eph. 1:3–4; 1 Peter 2:9; Titus 2:14.

seven

The Slave Market of Sin

In order to fully grasp what it means to be made a slave of Christ, we need to understand our previous slavery to sin—a universal reality. Remembering John Newton, the author of "Amazing Grace"—the most famous hymn ever written in the English language—is a good place to start. The lyrics tell of a sinner who was once lost, blind, and wretched before being found and rescued through no effort or merit of his own. As profound as they are personal, the words capture both the misery of sin and the joy of salvation. They express, in just a few short verses, the spiritual experience of the author, a man whose testimony is a remarkable witness to that very reality: God's amazing grace.

Newton was born in 1725, in London. His biography is one of the most well-known in church history—the story of how God transformed a blasphemous sailor and slave trader into a godly pastor and influential abolitionist. But what many do not know is that John Newton experienced the eighteenth-century slave trade from two opposite perspectives. Not only had he been the captain of a British slave ship (an occupation he would later deeply regret), but he had also been a slave himself, under the control of a cruel and abusive master, for fifteen months while living in Africa. Experiencing slave life first-hand, both as a slave and as the merchandiser of slaves, gave Newton unique insights into the world of slavery—insights that would impact him profoundly, both as a social reformer and as a theologian.

The story begins in 1744 when Newton was drafted against his wishes into Britain's Royal Navy and found himself bound for India as a sailor on the HMS *Harwich*. He was accustomed to ships because his father was a merchant ship captain. Yet, he found his time in the navy to be unbearable—due largely to his own insubordination and lack of discipline. When an opportunity came to leave, Newton didn't hesitate. Biographer Iain Murray recounts the event:

> When the fleet, heading south through the Atlantic, reached the island of Madeira, Newton was one morning lying in his hammock when a midshipman came in and cut the hammock down. Disgruntled, Newton arrived on the deck to find a fellow sailor about to be transferred from the *Harwich* to a merchant ship. The naval escorts, he discovered, required two trained seamen and were taking them from a merchantman. Two of the crew of the *Harwich* were to be given in exchange, but only one man had been selected for that purpose when Newton saw what was happening. At once he pleaded that he should be allowed to join the sailor about to leave, and probably thankful to be rid of him, the captain gave him leave to go. Barely a few minutes intervened between his being asleep in his hammock, and his hasty departure, with only a few clothes and one book.[1]

In this way, the young John Newton escaped from both the British navy and the long trip to India. He became a crew member of a merchant ship, a position he knew well from sailing with his father. Yet this experience would be different in at least one significant respect. For "he had boarded not just any ship, but a Guinea ship—a slave ship. He was only nineteen and little knew that his time in the slave trade would

---

1. Iain H. Murray, *Heroes* (Carlisle, PA: Banner of Truth, 2009), 90–91.

last nine long years and that he would experience things that would shape and change his life forever."[2]

Over the following months, the ship purchased slaves along Africa's western coast, for the purpose of transporting them to the West Indies and America before returning to Britain. But Newton would not accompany it to America. After meeting one of the ship's passengers—a man who had become wealthy through his own business pursuits on the African coast—Newton decided to stay in Africa and work for him. He was convinced that, like this man who had hired him, he could find quick riches if he stayed behind.

What followed was, by Newton's own account, the darkest and most miserable period of his life. Due to a series of events, including a severe sickness, he fell out of favor with both his new employer and the man's mistress. As a result, he was treated like a despised slave—"destitute of food and clothing, depressed to a degree beyond common wretchedness"[3]—such that even the natives "thought themselves too good to speak to me."[4] As Newton would later recall, "I was, in effect though without the name, a captive, and a slave myself; and was depressed to the lowest degree of human wretchedness."[5]

Years later, in one of his letters, Newton reflected on this part of his life:

---

2. Grant Gordon, "The Earlier Years of Newton and Ryland," 1–10, in John Newton, *Wise Counsel: John Newton's Letters to John Ryland Jr.*, ed. Grant Gordon (Carlisle, PA: Banner of Truth, 2009), 1.

3. John Newton, *An Authentic Narrative*, ed. Richard Cecil (Edinburgh: John Anderson, 1825), letter 5, 44.

4. Ibid., letter 5, 39.

5. John Newton, *The Works of John Newton*, 4 vols. (New Haven: Nathan Whiting, 1824), 4:553. This particular part comes from Newton's pamphlet entitled "Thoughts upon the African Slave Trade."

I had sometimes not a little difficulty to procure a draught of cold water when burning with a fever. My bed was a mat spread upon a board or chest, and a log of wood my pillow. When my fever left me, and my appetite returned, I would gladly have eaten, but there was no one gave unto me. . . . When I was very slowly recovering [from sickness], this woman [my master's mistress] would sometimes pay me a visit, not to pity or relieve, but to insult me. She would call me worthless and indolent, and compel me to walk; which, when I could hardly do, she would set her attendants to mimic my motion, to clap their hands, laugh, throw limes at me; or if they chose to throw stones, (as I think was the case once or twice), they were not rebuked; but, in general, though all who depended on her favour must join in her treatment, yet, when she was out of sight, I was rather pitied than scorned by the [lowest] of her slaves.[6]

While on a journey by ship with his master, Newton continued to receive similar ill treatment.

Whenever he [my master] left the vessel I was locked upon deck, with a pint of rice for my day's allowance; and if he stayed longer, I had no relief till his return. Indeed, I believe I should have been nearly starved, but for an opportunity of catching fish sometimes. . . . My whole suit was a shirt, a pair of trousers, a cotton handkerchief instead of a cap, and a cotton cloth, about two yards long, to supply the want of upper garments; and, thus accoutered [clothed], I have been exposed for twenty, thirty, perhaps near forty hours together, in incessant rains, accompanied with strong gales of wind, without the

6. Newton, *An Authentic Narrative*, letter 5, 42–43.

least shelter, when my master was on shore. I feel to this day some faint returns of the violent pains I then contracted. The excessive cold and wet I endured in that voyage, and so soon after I had recovered from a long sickness, quite broke my constitution and my spirits. The latter were soon restored; but the effects of the former still remain with me, as a needful *memento* of the service and wages of sin.[7]

Such was his condition—"living in hunger, and in thirst, and in nakedness, and the want of all things"[8]—that Newton would often hide himself from any potential visitors. He was, by his own account, "so poor a figure, that when a ship's boat came to the island, shame often constrained me to hide myself in the woods from the sight of strangers."[9] Eventually, after about a year's time, Newton's circumstances did improve when his master allowed him to work for a new employer. But that arrangement lasted only a few months, as the young man would soon be rescued. "Having many friends who were captains of ships, his father had urged those trading on the African coast to appeal for information about his son. Eventually, in February 1747, the captain of the *Greyhound* found him and took him on board."[10] As Newton explained in his letters, "Thus I was suddenly freed from a captivity of about fifteen months."[11]

At this point, Newton was still not a Christian. In fact, he maintained his reputation for excessive profanity and mischief, even among his fellow sailors! But God had His eye on Newton. Some months

---

7. Ibid., 43–44.

8. Ibid., letter 6, 47.

9. Ibid., 46.

10. Iain Murray, *Heroes*, 92.

11. Newton, *An Authentic Narrative*, letter 6, 51.

later, as the *Greyhound* was en route to Ireland, a violent storm brought this impenitent rebel to his senses, and in a moment of panic, he cried out to God for mercy. The ship survived, though almost miraculously so, and the crew eventually made it back home. Writing about this spiritual experience, Newton would recount years later:

> [I was] sincerely touched with a sense of the undeserved mercy I had received, in being brought safe through so many dangers. I was sorry for my past misspent life, and purposed an immediate reformation.... I acknowledged the Lord's mercy in pardoning what was past, but depended chiefly upon my own resolution to do better for the time to come. I had no Christian friend or faithful minister to advise me that my strength was no more than my righteousness. . . . Therefore I consider this as the beginning of my return to God, or rather of His return to me; but I cannot consider myself to have been a believer (in the full sense of the word) till a considerable time afterwards.[12]

When Newton returned to Britain, he continued to pursue the slave trade. In fact, he soon began a career as the captain of a slave ship. Given all he had just experienced, his decision to pursue this objectionable occupation is difficult to reconcile. The young sailor's conscience was still greatly underdeveloped[13] (by his own account, he was not yet a genuine believer), and his time in Africa combined with his years of sailing experience made him uniquely qualified for the position. Moreover, having landed a steady job as a sea captain, he was now able to pursue marriage to the love of his life, Polly. But notwithstanding

---

12. Cited from Gordon, "The Earlier Years of Newton and Ryland," 2.

13. Reflecting on those years, Newton admitted, "During the time I was engaged in the slave trade I never had the least scruple as to its lawfulness" (*The Works of John Newton*, 1:65).

his rationalization at the time, Newton would later look back on his involvement in the slave trade with deep sorrow and shame.

Over the next few years, he would lead a total of four slaving expeditions—the first as a first mate and the other three as the captain of his own ship. Though he did his best "to treat the slaves under [his] care with gentleness, and to consult their ease and convenience,"[14] Newton admitted to being "shocked with an employment that was perpetually conversant with chains, bolts, and shackles."[15] Even during this time in his life, he "often petitioned in [his] prayers, that the Lord in His own time would be pleased to fix [him] in a more humane calling."[16] When unexpected health problems forced him to stop sailing, Newton took a position in the customs office in the port of Liverpool. Nine years later, he would be ordained as a minister, a calling he would faithfully pursue until he was eighty-two.

In 1788, thirty-four years after leaving the slave trade, Newton publicly denounced it (and apologized for his part in it) in a pamphlet entitled "Thoughts upon the Slave Trade." The pamphlet was widely read and contributed greatly to the British abolitionist movement of the late 1700s. In it, Newton wrote: "I am bound in conscience to take shame to myself by a public confession, which, however sincere, comes too late to prevent or repair the misery and mischief to which I have, formerly, been accessory. I hope it will always be a subject of humiliating reflection to me, that I was once an active instrument in a business at which my heart now shudders."[17]

---

14. Cited from Gordon, "The Earlier Years of Newton," 2.

15. Newton, *Authentic Narrative*, letter 13, 96.

16. Ibid.

17. Newton, *The Works of John Newton*, 4:533.

Newton also preached against slavery and sought its abolishment. In a 1794 sermon, while recounting the social ills of his day, Newton told his flock:

I should be inexcusable, considering the share I have formerly had in that unhappy business, if, upon this occasion, I should omit to mention the African slave-trade. I do not rank this amongst our national sins; because I hope and believe, a very great majority of the nation, earnestly long for its suppression. But, hitherto, petty and partial interests prevail against the voice of justice, humanity, and truth. This enormity, however, is not sufficiently laid to heart. If you are justly shocked by what you hear of the cruelties practiced in France, you would perhaps be shocked much more, if you could fully conceive of the evils and miseries inseparable from this traffic, which I apprehend, not from hearsay, but from my own observation, are equal in atrocity, and perhaps superior in number, in the course of a single year, to any or all the worst actions which have been known in France since the commencement of their revolution.[18]

Several years later, in 1797, he would again tell his congregation: "I have more than once confessed with shame in this pulpit, the concern [participation] I had too long in the African slave-trade."[19]

Newton's influence, along with his friendship to William Wilberforce, helped the abolitionist cause in Britain reach its goal. In an 1805 letter to Wilberforce, the aged minister expressed his support:

---

18. John Newton, *The Works of the Rev. John Newton: Complete in One Volume* (London: Thomas Nelson, 1853), 860–61.

19. Ibid., 869.

I must attempt to express my thankfulness to the Lord and offer my congratulations to you for the success that He has so far been pleased to give your unwearied endeavours for the abolition of the slave trade. . . . Whether I, who am within two months of entering my eightieth year, shall live to see the accomplishment of that work, is known only to Him in whose hands are all our times and ways, but the hopeful prospect of its accomplishment will, I trust, give me daily satisfaction so long as my declining facilities are preserved.[20]

In February 1807, just ten months before Newton died, Parliament finally passed the Slave Trade Act, making that horrific trade illegal in the British Empire. The fact that Newton lived to see this notable victory is a fitting climax to his legacy. Newton's epitaph, which he wrote before he died, underscored his profound appreciation for that to which he owed everything—God's amazing grace:

JOHN NEWTON, Clerk
once an Infidel and Libertine,
a Servant of Slaves in Africa,
was, by the rich mercy
of our Lord and Saviour

JESUS CHRIST,

preserved, restored, pardoned,
and appointed to preach the faith
he had long laboured to destroy.

---

20. From a letter dated June 5, 1804, in Kevin Belmonte, *William Wilberforce: A Hero for Humanity* (Grand Rapids: Zondervan, 2007), 146.

Slavery to Sin

If anyone understood the horrors and abuses of the eighteenth-century slave trade, it was John Newton. He had experienced slavery from both sides—having lived as a slave in Africa, and having participated in the trade after returning home. As a minister, he had written about the abuses of slavery, and in the end, he was instrumental in bringing the British slave trade to its end. Christians today can rejoice in God's providential use of John Newton—not only by saving him personally from his wicked past but also by using him (along with William Wilberforce and others) to end one of modern history's great injustices.

As Newton came to realize, the British-American slave trade of his day was utterly unrighteous and unbiblical. The kidnapping or "man stealing" on which the entire system was built is clearly prohibited by both the Old and New Testaments (Ex. 21:16; 1 Tim. 1:10). Moreover, the racial prejudice it engendered has no place in the church, where all believers are comembers of the body of Christ (1 Cor. 12:13; Gal. 3:28). It is therefore no wonder that, as his years of ministry progressed, John Newton grew increasingly disgusted with that wicked institution and his involvement in it.

Nonetheless, Newton's unique testimony gave him a deep sense of appreciation for God's rescuing mercy in his life. His past experiences helped him understand what it truly meant to be a *slave of sin*—to be hopelessly oppressed and exploited by a wicked master. Even toward the end of his life, at age seventy-five, Newton would still write of his "state of wickedness and misery in Africa, which," he said, "has seldom been two hours together out of my waking thoughts."[21] He often

---

21. Newton, *Wise Counsel*, 380.

reflected on the harsh reality of his own enslavement, drawing parallels from his experience to the spiritual reality of sin's bondage. Perhaps no more striking parallel exists, at least in recent centuries, between the cruel wickedness of the British-American slave trade and the harsh oppression of slavery to sin.

Throughout his letters and hymns, Newton repeatedly contrasted bondage to sin with the redemption he received through Jesus Christ. He portrayed himself in his lost condition as "the willing slave of every evil"[22] and "Satan's blind slave"[23] who, if Christ had not rescued him, would have "been a captive still."[24] Newton's hymns—of which there are nearly three hundred—resound with the glorious theme of deliverance from his own wickedness.[25] Though he had once been a slave to the "madness, poison, [and] death" of sin, he had been liberated by the grace of God.

Newton remembered what it was like to be unconverted, to be one of those who "act as Satan bid," bound by "chains of guilt and sin." He knew that unbelievers are:

> *By nature how depraved,*
> *How prone to every ill,*
> *[Their] lives to Satan how enslaved,*
> *How obstinate [their] will.*

---

22. Newton, *The Works of John Newton* (Whiting), 1:27, from a letter dated January 17, 1763.

23. John Newton, "I Will Trust and Not Be Afraid," Book III, Hymn 37, in *Olney Hymns: In Three Parts* (London: Thomas Nelson, 1855), 289.

24. John Newton, "The Legion Dispossessed," Book I, Hymn 92, in *Olney Hymns*, 105–6.

25. The quotations that follow in this section come from John Newton's hymns in *Olney Hymns*. The hymns cited are: Book I: Hymns 109, 101, 118, 121, 122, 123; Book II: Hymns 21, 25, 29, 39, 56, 100; Book III: 76, 87. Slight adjustments have been made to the formatting of the hymns. British spellings have been replaced with American spellings, and abbreviated words have been spelled out in their entirety.

Their pitiful existence is "careless awhile they live in sin, enslaved to Satan's power." For in "the castle of the [unbelieving] human heart,"

> *[Satan] reigns,*
> *And keeps his goods in peace.*
> *The soul is pleased to wear his chains,*
> *Nor wishes a release.*

But Newton also knew that

> *Jesus [being] stronger far than he,*
> *In His appointed hour,*
> *Appears to set His people free*
> *From the usurper's power.*

Newton rejoiced in the fact that "Jesus rescues Satan's slaves," for

> *He sees us willing slaves,*
> *To sin and Satan's power;*
> *But with an outstretched arm He saves,*
> *In His appointed hour.*

We were "from sin and darkness freed" for Jesus "delivered [us] when bound." Though we were dead in our sins, God made us alive, such that "we begin to live indeed, when [we are] from our sin and bondage freed."

At the same time, Newton also understood the ethical implications of his liberty in Christ. Though he had been rescued from the evil oppression of sin, he now had a new Master, the Lord Jesus Christ. But unlike sin—the most wicked and cruel of all oppressors—Christ is the perfect Master, being righteous, just, gracious, and good. To submit to His will is pure joy. Therefore, Newton could exclaim:

> *Farewell world, thy gold is dross.*
> *Now I see the bleeding cross.*
> *Jesus died to set me free,*
> *From the law and sin and thee.*
> *He has dearly bought my soul,*
> *Lord accept and claim the whole.*
> *To Thy will I all resign,*
> *Now no more my own but Thine.*

Elsewhere he wrote:

> *Now Lord I would be Thine alone.*
> *Come take possession of Thine own.*
> *For Thou hast set me free,*
> *Released from Satan's hard command.*
> *See all my powers waiting stand,*
> *To be employed by Thee.*

Thus,

> *The rebel soul that once withstood,*
> *The Savior's kindest call,*
> *Rejoices now by grace subdued*
> *To serve Him with her all.*

Having been rescued from the slavish bonds of sin, Newton was eager to obey Christ with all of his heart. In a hymn entitled "We Were

Pharaoh's Bondmen," Newton compared the Christian's deliverance from sin to Israel's deliverance from Egypt. Like Pharaoh, sin is the harshest of taskmasters. But Christians, like the Israelites, can rejoice in being rescued by God's grace.

> *Beneath the tyrant Satan's yoke*
> *Our souls were long oppressed;*
> *'Till grace our galling fetters broke,*
> *And gave the weary rest.*
> *Jesus, in that important hour,*
> *His mighty arm made known;*
> *He ransomed us by price and power,*
> *And claimed us for His own.*
> *Now, freed from bondage, sin, and death,*
> *We walk in wisdom's ways;*
> *And wish to spend our every breath*
> *In wonder, love, and praise.*
> *Ere long, we hope with Him to dwell*
> *In yonder world above;*
> *And now we only live to tell*
> *The riches of His love.*

eight

Bound, Blind, and Dead

We have already noted some of the significant differences between the slavery of 1700s British imperialism and that of the first-century Roman world. Most significantly, Roman slavery was not racially defined, such that first-century slaves were generally indistinguishable from free men both in physical appearance and in dress. Moreover, Roman slaves often had the opportunity to earn their freedom—eventually becoming citizens and even masters themselves. Additionally, the slaves of a good master enjoyed a stable and relatively comfortable life, and the slaves of important people often possessed a certain degree of their own prestige and influence. First-century slaves might be highly educated or trained as specialists in their fields, allowing them to function in the same capacity as free persons. In fact, some slaves even worked as doctors, teachers, or philosophers in the employ of their masters. Though Roman society never viewed slavery as the ideal, the institution did not generally carry the same stigma that is associated with the eighteenth-century slave trade.[1]

Nevertheless, Roman literature does provide examples of injustices inflicted upon slaves by cruel and unjust masters. In the same way

---

1. Along these lines, S. Scott Bartchy notes, "The first century A.D., then, was a time in which the living conditions for those in slavery were improving. Legal action and public opinion supported better treatment of slaves.... [M]ost slaves in the first century were born in the households of their owners, and they were given training for personal and public tasks of increasing importance and sensitivity. They were treated accordingly" (*First-Century Slavery* [Eugene, OR: Wipf and Stock Publishers, 2002], 71).

that John Newton's experiences affected his theological perspective,[2] accounts like these would have given first-century Christians a vivid understanding of the pain and misery that comes from enslavement to a wicked tyrant. History professor S. Scott Bartchy gives one such example:

> In his discussion of the futility of anger, Seneca reports that a very rich Roman freedman, Vedius Pollio, allowed his flesh-eating fish to dine on slaves. One day, as a slave carelessly broke a crystal vase in the presence of some guests, including Augustus Caesar, Vedius commanded that the slave be thrown into the fish-pond. In answer to the slave's cry for help, Augustus commanded that all the crystal owned by Vedius be brought before him, broken up and thrown into the grisly pond instead of the slave.[3]

Though this account represents the exception and not the rule, it provides a vivid illustration of the kind of extreme cruelty that wicked masters could inflict upon their slaves.

Over time, Roman law began to protect slaves from such circumstances. Around AD 61, the *Lex Petronia*:

---

2. In *Sixty-Six Letters to a Clergyman and His Family* (London: Simpkin, Marshall, & Co., 1844), Newton recognized the hardship that the slaves of unjust masters would have endured in New Testament times: "Servants, in the apostles' times, were slaves. . . . The servants of heathen masters had doubtless much to suffer; yet the apostle expects that these poor slaves would adorn the doctrine of God their Savior, and follow His example in all things" (160–61).

3. Bartchy, *First-Century Slavery*, 69. In his footnote (n235), the author explains that "this is an unusual story which shows not only the shocking and terrible side of slavery but also the official interest in overcoming it." The author went on to explain that, from simply an economic perspective, masters had much more to gain by treating their slaves well than by treating them cruelly.

prohibited owners from exposing their slaves to fight with wild beasts without permission from the competent magistrate (approval was given only when very bad conduct was proven). Antonius Pius, Emperor during the middle of the second century A.D., proclaimed that if a slave took refuge at a statue of the Emperor, the provincial governor was to hold an enquiry; if he was convinced of the owner's cruelty, the owner was to be forced to sell all his slaves.[4]

But the need for laws like these indicates that cruelty to slaves did occur in the Roman world.[5]

Early Christians would have been well aware of the abuses a slave could suffer at the hands of an unjust owner. Many first-century believers were slaves themselves,[6] and some of them were subjected to harsh and unfair treatment. In light of this, Peter instructed them, "Be submissive to your masters with all respect, not only to those who are good and gentle, but also to those who are unreasonable. For this finds favor, if for the sake of conscience toward God a person bears up under sorrows when suffering unjustly" (1 Peter 2:18–19).

It is against this cultural backdrop that the New Testament speaks of slavery to sin and of sin's reign in the human heart. Sin is the vilest, most dreadful master imaginable (cf. Gen. 4:7)—a reality which would not have been lost on first-century believers.[7] They would have

---

4. Ibid., 71, n. 247.

5. For a survey of Greco-Roman writings that evidence the cruelty with which slaves were sometimes treated, see Thomas Wiedemann, *Greek & Roman Slavery* (New York: Routledge, 1988), 9–11, 167–87.

6. See Ephesians 6:5–9; Colossians 3:22–25; Titus 2:9–10; Philemon 1:15–16.

7. Commenting on Romans 6, Leon Morris (in *Romans, Pillar New Testament Commentary* [Grand Rapids: Eerdmans, 1998], 261) says of Paul's readers, "They were familiar with slavery, and Paul is reasoning from the well-known fact that a slave was completely at the disposal of

naturally drawn parallels from the worst abuses in their culture, understanding the total subjugation that such slavery entailed.

As we saw in chapter 2, they could also look to the Old Testament for illustrations of such oppression, the foremost of which was the pharaoh of the Exodus. By the first century, it was not uncommon to think of redemption in terms of Israel's deliverance from Egypt.[8] Such provided a natural parallel to the Christian's redemption from sin. In the same way that Pharaoh was a brutal tyrant, daily afflicting his Israelite work force with hardship and bitterness, "sin too is a harsh taskmaster that ruthlessly uses [its slaves] but fails to offer any real reward."[9] Thus, whether they considered the ill-treatment of slaves in their own culture or the plight of Israelite slaves in ancient Egypt, first-century believers would have readily understood the imagery of slavery to sin.

Sin is a cruel tyrant. It is the most devastating and degenerating power ever to afflict the human race, such that the entire creation "groans and suffers the pains of childbirth together until now" (Rom. 8:22). It corrupts the entire person—infecting the soul, polluting the mind, defiling the conscience, contaminating the affections, and

---

his master. . . . For Paul the basic assumption is that all are slaves before they become believers in Christ; they are not free to do as they will, for they are subject to the bondage of sin."

8. F. Büchsel, under "λυτρόω," in *Theological Dictionary of the New Testament*, edited by Gerhard Kittel, and translated and edited by Geoffrey W. Bromiley (Grand Rapids: Eerdmans, 1967), explains that "redemption in later Jewish usage is always the redemption of Israel from the dominion of Gentile peoples, often the exodus from Egypt, but also the many other redemptions in Jewish history, e.g., from oppression by Antiochus Epiphanes IV" (4:350). For more on the New Testament connection between the Israelites as slaves in Egypt and unbelievers as slaves to sin, see John Byron, *Slavery Metaphors in Early Judaism and Pauline Christianity* (Tubingen, Germany: J. C. B. Mohr, 2003), 229.

9. Lawrence O. Richards, *Bible Reader's Companion* (Colorado Springs: David C. Cook, 1991), 53.

poisoning the will.[10] It is the life-destroying, soul-condemning cancer that festers and grows in every unredeemed human heart like an incurable gangrene.

But unbelievers are not just infected by sin; they are enslaved by it. Jesus told His listeners in John 8:34, "Truly, truly I say to you, everyone who commits sin is the slave of sin." The apostle Peter likewise described false teachers as "slaves of corruption; for by what a man is overcome, by this he is enslaved" (2 Peter 2:19). Using this same imagery, Paul reminded the Romans that, before their salvation, they "were slaves of sin" (6:17). Every human being, until the moment of redemption, is under the domain of darkness and the dominion of sin. The unbeliever is wholly corrupted by the bondage of his fallen condition and utterly unable to free himself from it.

Not surprisingly, the very notion of such absolute enslavement (a doctrine commonly known as "total depravity" or "total inability"[11]) is repugnant to the fallen human heart. In fact, no doctrine is more hated by unbelievers than this one, and even some Christians find it so offensive that they zealously attack it.[12] Though the doctrine of total depravity is often the most attacked and minimized of the doctrines

---

10. See Jeremiah 44:15–17; John 3:19–21; Romans 1:21; 2 Corinthians 7:1; Titus 1:15.

11. It is important to note that "total depravity" does not mean that every sinner is as cruel or vicious as it is possible to be. Obviously, that is not the case. Not every sinner is a mass murderer or rapist. In fact, some sinners seem to be relatively good people, compared to others. But the Bible is clear about the *extent* of every sinner's fallenness. There is no part of the sinner's nature or being that has not been entirely tainted by sin. Thus, when we speak of "total depravity," we are speaking of the full extent to which every sinner has been contaminated by the effects of sin. That contamination defines the sinner as spiritually dead, totally unable to respond positively to spiritual truth.

12. For more on the doctrine of total depravity see my chapters "The Sinner Neither Willing nor Able" (pp. 81–98), in *Proclaiming a Cross-Centered Theology* (Wheaton, IL: Crossway, 2009); and "Man's Radical Corruption" (pp. 129–40), in *John Calvin: A Heart for Devotion, Doctrine, & Doxology* (Orlando: Reformation Trust, 2008).

of grace, it is the most distinctly Christian doctrine because it is foundational to a right understanding of the gospel (in which God initiates everything and receives all the glory). The neglect of this doctrine within American evangelicalism has resulted in all kinds of errors, including both the watered-down gospel and the seeker-driven pragmatism of the church growth movement. But the Scripture is clear: unless the Spirit of God gives spiritual life, all sinners are completely unable to change their fallen nature or to rescue themselves from sin and divine judgment. They can neither initiate nor accomplish any aspect of their redemption. Even the supposed "good things" that unbelievers do are like filthy rags before a holy God (Isa. 64:6). Contrast that with every other religious system, in which people are told that through their own efforts they *can* achieve some level of righteousness, thereby contributing to their salvation. Nothing could be further from the truth.

One of the dominant features of universal human fallenness is the sinner's deception about his true condition. Motivated by pride, the depraved mind thinks itself much better than it really is. But God's Word cuts through that deception like a sharp sword, diagnosing sinful men as incurably sick, rebellious by nature, and incapable of any spiritual good.

As slaves to sin, all unbelievers are hostile toward God and unable to please Him in any respect.[13] Their total inability is underscored by the fact that they are not just bound to sin; they are also *blinded* by sin and *dead* in it. They are "darkened in their understanding" (Eph. 4:18) and cannot comprehend spiritual truth because "the god of this world

---

13. See Jeremiah 13:23; Romans 8:7–8; 14:23; Hebrews 11:6. Along these lines, the Westminster Confession of Faith (chap. 9, § 3) states, "Man, by his fall into a state of sin, hath wholly lost all ability of will to any spiritual good accompanying salvation; so as a natural man, being altogether averse from that good, and dead in sin, is not able, by his own strength, to convert himself, or to prepare himself thereunto."

[Satan] has blinded the minds of the unbelieving so that they might not see the light of the gospel of the glory of Christ" (2 Cor. 4:4).[14] Furthermore, unbelievers are "dead in [their] trespasses and sins" (Eph. 2:1), "dead in [their] transgressions" (Col. 2:13), "dead even while [they live]" (1 Tim. 5:6). In the same way that a blind man cannot give himself sight or a dead man raise himself to life, so the sinner is totally unable to impart to himself either spiritual understanding or eternal life. Like Lazarus lying motionless in the tomb, the unredeemed soul remains lifeless until the voice of God commands it, "Come forth!" Noting the parallels between the raising of Lazarus and the miracle of salvation, Charles Spurgeon observed:

> [T]he raising of Lazarus stands at the head of the wonderful series of miracles with which our Lord astonished and instructed the people. Yet I am not in error when I assert that it is a type of what the Lord Jesus is constantly doing at this hour in the realm of mind and spirit. Did he raise the naturally dead? So does he still raise the spiritually dead! Did he bring back a body from corruption? So does he still deliver men from loathsome sins![15]

---

14. Cf. John 8:43–44; 1 Cor. 2:14. Satan is the ruler of this wicked world system (John 12:31; 2 Cor. 4:4; Eph. 2:2) and the father of all "the sons of disobedience" (Eph. 5:6; cf. Matt. 13:38; 1 John 3:10). Known as "a murderer from the beginning" (John 8:44), "the father of lies" (John 8:44), the "evil one" (John 17:15; 1 John 5:19; cf. Matt. 13:19), and the "son of perdition" / "son of destruction" (John 17:12; 2 Thess. 2:3), he "prowls around like a roaring lion, seeking someone to devour" (1 Peter 5:8). Though the devil appears as an angel of light (2 Cor. 11:14), claiming to offer satisfaction in exchange for compliance to his demands (see Matthew 4:8–10), his temptations are nothing more than fiery arrows of spiritual destruction (Eph. 6:16; cf. 1 John 2:15–17).

15. Charles Spurgeon, "Unbinding Lazarus," sermon no. 1776, *Metropolitan Tabernacle Pulpit* (Pasadena, TX: Pilgrim Press, 1985), 30:219.

The story of Lazarus not only demonstrates Christ's divine power over death (both physical and spiritual); it also illustrates the converse theological truth—namely, that the dead cannot raise themselves. Apart from Christ's miraculous intervention, Lazarus's body would have remained lifeless in the tomb. All of humanity is a race of Lazaruses.[16] Until God miraculously intervenes, they remain spiritually dead, helplessly enslaved to the power and corruption of sin, "having no hope and without God in the world" (Eph. 2:12). Or as Spurgeon said it, "Through the fall, and through our own sin, the nature of man has become so debased, so depraved, and corrupt, that it is impossible for him to come to Christ without the assistance of God the Holy Spirit. . . . [Man's] nature is so corrupt that he has neither the will nor the power to come to Christ unless drawn by the Spirit."[17]

To make matters worse, the Bible teaches that unbelievers wholeheartedly love their sin. They are not only utterly *unable* to free themselves from its corruption; they are also obstinately *unwilling* to do so. As Jesus told the religious leaders of His day, "You search the Scriptures because you think that in them you have eternal life; it is these that testify about Me; and you are *unwilling* to come to Me so that you may have life" (John 5:39–40, emphasis added). Having inherited a fallen nature from Adam, sinful human beings are "by nature children of wrath" (Eph. 2:3), characterized by hard hearts, depraved minds,

---

16. On this point, author Duane Edward Spencer noted, "Just as Lazarus would never have heard the voice of Jesus, nor would he have ever 'come to Jesus,' without first being given life by our Lord, so all men 'dead in trespasses and sins' must first be given life by God before they can 'come to Christ.' Since dead men cannot *will* to receive life, but can be raised from the dead only by the power of God, so the natural man cannot of his own (mythical) 'free will' *will* to have eternal life (cf. John 10:26–28)" (Spencer, *Tulip: The Five Points of Calvinism in the Light of Scripture* [Grand Rapids: Baker], 28).

17. Charles Spurgeon, "Human Inability," *New Park Street Pulpit*, 4 vols. (London: Alabaster and Passmore, 1859), 4:138.

defiled consciences, and prideful actions that are hostile toward God.[18] As the Lord explained to His followers, "That which proceeds out of the man, that is what defiles the man. For from within, out of the heart of men, proceed the evil thoughts, fornications, thefts, murders, adulteries, deeds of coveting and wickedness, as well as deceit, sensuality, envy, slander, pride and foolishness. All these evil things proceed from within and defile the man" (Mark 7:20–23).

The apostle Paul similarly described the unbeliever's condition in Romans 3:10–12, emphasizing the sinner's unwillingness to come to God:

> *There is none righteous, no, not one;*
> *There is none who understands;*
> *There is none who seeks after God.*
> *They have all gone out of the way;*
> *They have together become unprofitable;*
> *There is none who does good, no, not one.* (NKJV)

Rather than pursuing God and His righteousness, unredeemed sinners gladly exchange "the truth of God for a lie" (Rom. 1:25), having "given themselves over to sensuality for the practice of every kind of impurity with greediness" (Eph. 4:19). They are "lovers of self, lovers of money, [and] lovers of pleasure rather than lovers of God" (2 Tim. 3:2, 4), perpetually seeking to indulge the desires of their flesh. Moreover, they are under the control and dominion of Satan, as Martin Luther explained in his treatise *On the Bondage of the Will*:

---

18. Regarding man's sin nature, see Psalm 51:5; Romans 3:23; 5:12, 15–17; 1 Corinthians 15:21. Regarding the corrupting effects of sin, see Psalm 143:2; Jeremiah 17:9; Romans 1:28; 5:10; 8:7; Ephesians 2:1–3; 4:18; Titus 1:15; 3:1–3.

Satan is the prince of the world, and, according to the testimonies of Christ and Paul, rules in the wills and minds of those men who are his captives and servants. . . . [It] is plainly proved by scriptures neither ambiguous nor obscure—that Satan, is by far the most powerful and crafty prince of this world; (as I said before,) under the reigning power of whom, the human will, being no longer free nor in its own power, but the servant of sin and of Satan, can will nothing but that which its prince wills. And he will not permit it to will anything good: though, even if Satan did not reign over it, sin itself, of which man is the slave, would sufficiently harden it to prevent it from willing good.[19]

Of course, those under Satan's dominion will share his same demise of eternal destruction. Though sin promises satisfaction and life to its slaves, its reward is in actuality the exact opposite—misery in this life and condemnation in the next.[20]

The astonishing reality is that even if the sinner could change the condition of his heart—which Scripture teaches is impossible (Jer. 13:23)—no unbeliever would ever will to do so. Left to his own natural reason and volition, the unredeemed sinner will always choose slavery to sin over obedience to God. Until the Lord intervenes, the sinner is neither able nor willing to abandon his sin and serve God in righteousness. Both his will and his reason are utterly corrupt. Luther makes the point through a series of rhetorical questions:

What then can [a sinner's] reason propose that is right, who is thus blind and ignorant? What can the will choose that is good, which

---

19. Martin Luther, *On the Bondage of the Will*, trans. Henry Cole (London: T. Bensley, 1823), 293, 295. Cf. Gal. 4:8; Eph. 2:2.

20. Cf. Ezek. 18:4; Matt. 5:29; Rom. 6:23; 8:13; Gal. 6:8; James 1:15; Rev. 20:10–15.

is thus evil and impotent? Nay, what can the will pursue, where the reason can propose nothing, but the darkness of its own blindness and ignorance? And where the reason is thus erroneous, and the will averse, what can the [unbelieving] man either do or attempt, that is good![21]

The answer, of course, is *nothing*. The contaminated mind and corrupted will of the unconverted heart are only capable of choosing sin. The unredeemed soul therefore "is compulsively bound to the service of sin, and cannot will anything good."[22] Apart from divine intervention, the slave of sin remains in an utterly helpless and hopeless situation. He is not only powerless to free himself, but he wears his chains with willing eagerness.

---

21. Luther, *On the Bondage of the Will*, 320.

22. Ibid., 125. In this section, Luther is showing the fallacy of Erasmus's use of the term "free will." In the process, Luther evidences his own understanding of total depravity.

nine

Saved from Sin,
Slaved by Grace

It is from slavery to sin that God saves His elect, rescuing them from the domain of darkness and transferring them as His own slaves into the kingdom of His Son (Col. 1:13). When we loved nothing but ourselves and our sin, God first loved us, such that we might respond to Him in faith.[1] As the apostle John explains, "In this is love, not that we loved God, but that He loved us and sent His Son to be the propitiation for our sins. . . . We love Him because He first loved us" (1 John 4:10, 19 NKJV). In saving us from slavery to sin, God initiated and accomplished everything. Were it not for His purposeful intervention, we would still be helplessly in bondage to sin.

It is important to note that in Roman times, slaves did not choose their masters; rather, masters chose their slaves. This point is made abundantly clear by descriptions of the ancient Roman slave market, where slaves were entirely subject to the opinions and decisions of potential buyers.[2] As Francis Lyall explains,

As slaves were things, mere commercial assets, they might be bought

---

1. Passages such as John 4:10; Acts 11:17–18; Ephesians 2:8; Philippians 1:29; 2 Peter 1:1; 2 Timothy 2:25; and Titus 3:5 indicate that a saving, repentant faith is the gift of God, not the product of man's effort.

2. Keith Bradley explains that, without any say in the matter, slaves "seem for the most part to have endured the proceedings in silence" (*Slavery and Society at Rome* [Cambridge University Press, 1994], 56).

and sold or their ownership otherwise transferred without any say on their part. The transfer of a slave was a technical matter, but it would often be occasioned by a purchase. It is interesting therefore to find two instances of such imagery in 1 Corinthians, a letter addressed to the church in a city that housed an important slave market. In 1 Corinthians 6:20 and 7:23 we learn that we are "bought with a price." . . . [Significantly,] in a question of slave and purchase, the will of the slave was totally unimportant.[3]

In the Roman slave market, decisions regarding the slave's future rested solely in the hands of the purchaser, not the one being sold. Similarly, the Bible teaches that God has chosen His slaves by His own sovereign, independent, electing choice. In fact, He elected them to be His slaves before they were born, and even before the world was created.[4]

As those chosen by God, believers were "purchased with [Christ's] own blood" (Acts 20:28),[5] predestined to be freed from slavery to sin and ushered into the household of God.[6] He pursued us even though we did not seek Him, drawing us to Himself and snatching us from the clutches and condemnation of sin. Like Paul, we were "laid hold of by Christ Jesus" (Phil. 3:12), becoming His willing captives, His

---

3. Francis Lyall, *Slaves, Citizens, Sons: Legal Metaphors in the Epistles* (Grand Rapids: Academie Books, 1984), 38–39. Additionally, Murray J. Harris draws a connection between 1 Corinthians 6:20 and 7:23 and "the Old Testament concept of God's 'redemption-acquisition' of the people of Israel after their Egyptian bondage (*e.g.*, Exod. 6:6; Ps. 74:2) to become his treasured possession (Exod. 19:5–6; Deut. 26:18; Mal. 3:17)" (*Slave of Christ* [Downers Grove, IL: Intervarsity Press, 1999], 122).

4. Cf. Rom. 9:11; Eph. 1:4; 2 Thess. 2:13; 2 Tim. 1:9; Titus 1:2.

5. See also 1 Peter 1:18–19; Rev. 5:9; 14:4.

6. Cf. Gal. 6:10; Eph. 2:19; Heb. 3:6; 1 Peter 2:5; 4:17.

joyful prisoners, and part of the people for His own possession.[7] We are those who belong to Him, not because we chose Him but because He chose us.

But unlike the Roman slave market—where slaves were selected based on their positive qualities, like strength, health, and physical appearance—God chose His slaves with the full knowledge of their weaknesses and failures. We "were not many wise according to the flesh, not many mighty, not many noble; but God has chosen the foolish things of the world to shame the wise, and God has chosen the weak things of the world to shame the things which are strong" (1 Cor. 1:26–27). Indeed, He mercifully elected us to salvation in spite of ourselves, saving us—not because of any inherent goodness in us—but according to His own eternal purposes and for the sake of His glory.

The New Testament is replete with examples of God's electing and initiating work in salvation. In John 15:16, Jesus told His disciples, "You did not choose Me but I chose you, and appointed you that you would go and bear fruit, and that your fruit would remain, so that whatever you ask of the Father in My name He may give to you." In Acts 2:39, Peter emphasized that the promise of salvation extended to "as many as the Lord our God will call to Himself." Acts 13:48 reports that, in response to Paul's missionary work among the Gentiles, "as many as had been appointed to eternal life believed." A couple chapters later, we learn that Lydia believed only after "the Lord opened her heart to respond to the things spoken by Paul" (Acts 16:14). In each instance, it was God who did the work of choosing, calling, appointing,

---

7. Cf. Rom. 16:7; 2 Cor. 2:14; Eph. 3:1; Col. 4:10; 2 Tim. 1:8; Titus 2:14; Philem. 1, 9, 23; and 1 Peter 2:9. The term "fellow prisoner" in Romans 16:7, Colossians 4:10, and Philemon 23 is literally "fellow prisoner of war." It is likely that Paul was using this in a figurative sense, to include himself and these men as fellow captives in Christ's service (cf. Harris, *Slave of Christ*, 117).

and opening the heart. Such is still the case whenever a soul is saved, for the new birth always comes, not by "the will of the flesh nor of the will of man, but of God" (John 1:13).

God's will in salvation is singular, dependent on nothing other than His uninfluenced, free, electing choice. Therefore, the Holy Spirit works where He wills, the Son gives life to whomever He wishes, and unless the Father draws them, unbelievers cannot come to Christ.[8] When we were bound in our sins, the Son set us free (John 8:36). When we were blinded by unbelief, God "shone in our hearts to give the Light of the knowledge of the glory of God in the face of Christ" (2 Cor. 4:6). When we were dead in our trespasses and sins, He "made us alive together with Christ" (Eph. 2:5). He is the one who initiated every aspect of the work of salvation in our hearts, such that we can take no credit for anything in our salvation.[9] All the glory goes to Him.

In salvation, the triune God sovereignly acts upon those whom He wills to rescue, imparting life to dead hearts and sight to darkened minds. Salvation, then, "does not depend on the man who wills or the man who runs, but on God who has mercy" (Rom. 9:16). Just as we did not choose to be born in the physical sense, so we did not choose to be born from above (John 3:3–8). You and I believed the gospel, not because we were wiser or more righteous than anyone else but because God graciously intervened, opening our hearts to heed His Word and believe. There is no room for subtle pride on our part, only gratitude; God's sole work in the redemption of sinners means that He receives all of the praise.

Of course, the doctrine of sovereign election does not negate or

---

8. John 3:7; 5:21; 6:44, 65; cf. Matt. 11:27.

9. Cf. Phil. 1:6 and 1 Cor. 1:29–31.

contradict the responsibility of the sinner to turn from sin and trust Christ as Savior and Lord.[10] The gospel calls all men to faith and repentance. But as we have seen, the sinful heart hates God and, given the choice, will always choose sin. Thankfully, God's sovereign grace includes not only the gift of salvation but also the repentant faith necessary for receiving that gift.[11] Thus, while sinners are wholly responsible for rejecting the gospel, God alone deserves the credit for the salvation of believers—having initiated, accomplished, and provided everything, including the means by which believers are able to respond to the gospel. As Richard Baxter so vividly expressed, "So then, let 'Deserved' be written on the floor of hell but on the door of heaven and life, 'The Free Gift.'"[12]

The apostle Paul repeatedly underscored the reality of divine predestination in his epistles, noting both God's electing choice and His effectual call.[13] He encouraged the Thessalonians, for example, with these words: "But we should always give thanks to God for you, brethren beloved by the Lord, *because God has chosen you from the beginning for salvation through sanctification* by the Spirit and faith in the truth. It was for this *He called you through our gospel*, that you may gain the glory of our Lord Jesus Christ" (2 Thess. 2:13–14, emphasis added).

In his letters to Timothy and Titus, the apostle even cited God's electing work as an incentive for his own endurance. He said to Timothy, "I endure all things for the sake of those who are chosen" (2 Tim. 2:10) and similarly explained to Titus that he was a slave of

---

10. Cf. Ezek. 18:23, 32; 33:11; John 3:18,19, 36; 5:40; 2 Thess. 2:10–12; Rev. 22:17.

11. Both faith (Eph. 2:8) and repentance (2 Tim. 2:25) are the gift of God.

12. Richard Baxter, *The Saints' Everlasting Rest*, cited in John MacArthur, *The Glory of Heaven* (Wheaton, IL: Crossway, 1996), 171.

13. Cf. Rom. 8:29–30, 33; Eph. 1:3–11; Col. 3:12; 1 Thess. 1:4.

God and an apostle of Christ "for the faith of those chosen of God" (Titus 1:1). Paul also included himself in the company of God's elect, noting that God "has saved us and called us with a holy calling, not according to our works, but according to His own purpose and grace which was granted us in Christ Jesus from all eternity" (2 Tim. 1:9).

Paul was not alone in his understanding of God's electing work in salvation. Other New Testament writers highlighted these very same realities. The author of Hebrews explained that Christ died so that "those who have been called may receive the promise of the eternal inheritance" (9:15). James noted that our salvation resulted from "the exercise of His will" when "He brought us forth by the word of truth" (James 1:18). Peter wrote his first epistle "to those . . . who are chosen according to the foreknowledge of God the Father, by the sanctifying work of the Spirit, to obey Jesus Christ and be sprinkled with His blood" (1 Peter 1:1–2).[14] John referred to a lady as "chosen" (2 John 1:13). And Jude, similarly, opened his letter with these words: "To those who are the called, beloved in God the Father, and kept for Jesus Christ" (v. 1).

The resounding chorus of Scripture reiterates this inescapable conclusion: God is the one who chooses to have "mercy on whom He desires" (Rom. 9:18). He initiates and accomplishes the work of salvation for those whom He predestined in eternity past. He calls them to Himself, granting them faith and repentance, and redeeming them from their slavery to sin. Consequently, believers are rightly designated as "the elect, whom He chose" (Mark 13:20), for we could not have loved Him unless He first loved us.

---

14. The word *foreknowledge* does not refer to a mere awareness of what will happen in the future, but a predetermination of what will happen. It speaks of planning, not simply observing (cf. Jer. 1:5; Acts 2:23). In this context, it indicates that God pre-thought and predestined each Christian's relationship with Him.

Bought with a Price

But how does God rescue those slaves of sin whom He has chosen for Himself? The New Testament answers this question with the doctrine of *redemption*—a concept that again borrows from the imagery of both the Roman slave market and Israel's exodus from slavery in Egypt.

Scripture uses two Greek words to convey the truth of redemption.[15] The first is *agorazō*, which, along with its related compound *exagorazō*, means "to buy" or "to purchase." The word derives from *agora*, meaning "marketplace," and speaks of buying or trading, and "especially of purchasing a slave with a view to his freedom."[16] Used figuratively, its meaning was "based on the analogy of religious law which in reality bestowed freedom on a slave purchased by a divinity."[17] From a theological perspective, it refers to the spiritual purchase of redemption, in which a price was paid to buy sinners out of their slavery. Thus, in the New Testament, "Christ is said to have purchased his disciples [having] made them, as it were, his private property. . . . He is also said to have bought them for God by shedding his blood."[18]

---

15. *The Evangelical Dictionary of Theology* (*EDT*) explains that redemption is "conveyed in the New Testament by the *agorazo* and *lyo* word groups. These terms have in mind the context of a marketplace transaction with reference to the purchase of goods or the releasing of slaves. In using these words, New Testament writers sought to represent Jesus' saving activity in terms that convey deliverance from bondage. Most of these words infer deliverance from captivity by means of a ransom price paid" (R. David Rightmire, "Redeem, Redemption," in *EDT*, Walter A. Elwell, ed. [Grand Rapids: Baker, 1996], 664–65).

16. W. E. Vine, commenting on "*exagorazō*" in *Expository Dictionary of New Testament Words* (Old Tappan, NJ: Fleming H. Revell Company, 1966), 263.

17. William F. Arndt and F. Wilbur Gingrich, commenting on "*agorazō*" in *A Greek-English Lexicon of the New Testament* (Chicago: Chicago University Press, 1969), 12.

18. Carl Ludwig Wilibald Grimm, commenting on "*agorazō*," in *Greek-English Lexicon of the New Testament*, trans. Joseph Henry Thayer (Grand Rapids: Zondervan, 1970), 8. Cf. John 17:9–10; 1 Cor. 6:20; Gal. 3:13; Rev. 5:9; 14:3–4.

The other Greek term for redemption is *lytroō* (and its related forms), referring specifically to "the ransom money [paid] for the manumission of slaves."[19] For those "sold into bondage to sin" (Rom. 7:14), a category that includes all of Adam's fallen descendants, redemption is the only means of rescue from sin's damning mastery. Only those who have been bought with a price, being ransomed through Christ's substitutionary death on the cross,[20] can rejoice in knowing that they have been fully forgiven. By God's grace, on account of Christ's atoning sacrifice, they have been freed from sin, Satan, and death.[21] As the author of Hebrews explains, the Son of God came so "that through death He might render powerless him who had the power of death, that is, the devil, and might free those who through fear of death were subject to slavery all their lives" (2:14–15).

The glorious theme of redemption—that believers were purchased by our Lord through His death—echoes throughout the New Testament.[22] But unlike the slaves of Roman times, we "were not redeemed with perishable things like silver or gold from [our] futile way of life" (1 Peter 1:18), nor were we redeemed through "the blood of

---

19. Arndt and Gingrich, commenting on "λύτρον" in *A Greek-English Lexicon of the New Testament*, 483.

20. Cf. Matt. 20:28; Mark 10:45; 1 Cor. 6:20; 7:23; 2 Cor. 5:21; Col. 2:14; 1 Tim. 2:6.

21. We must be careful not to press the ransom metaphor too far, as if to conclude that Christ paid some sort of ransom to sin or to Satan in order to free the slaves of sin. Christ died for God, such that His substitutionary death appeased God's wrath and satisfied God's justice, thereby making full atonement for the sins of those for whom He died. F. Büchsel, commenting on "λύτρον," in *Theological Wordbook of the New Testament*, edited by Gerhard Kittel, and translated and edited by Geoffrey W. Bromiley (Grand Rapids: Eerdmans, 1967) (IV, 344), observes that there is "no doubt but that God is the recipient of the ransom. Jesus serves God when He dies, and God inexorably demands suffering from His Son. God smites Him. All possibility that Satan might receive the ransom is thus ruled out. . . . [Sinners must] be liberated from indebtedness to God."

22. E.g., Rom. 3:24; Eph. 1:7; Col. 1:14.

goats and calves" (Heb. 9:12). Rather, our redemption is Jesus Christ Himself,[23] who in death "gave Himself for us to redeem us from every lawless deed, and to purify for Himself a people for His own possession, zealous for good deeds" (Titus 2:14). Now, as His possession, we who were formerly slaves to sin are slaves of a new Lord and Master.

Our redemption in Christ results in both *freedom* from sin and *forgiveness* for sin. Not only are we liberated from bondage to our former master; we are also exempt from sin's deadly consequences—namely, the eternal wrath of God. As Paul exclaimed in Romans 8:1–2, "Therefore there is now no condemnation for those who are in Christ Jesus. For the law of the Spirit of life in Christ Jesus has set you free from the law of sin and of death." Because we are in Him, all of our sins—past, present, and future—have been "forgiven [us] for His name's sake" (1 John 2:12).[24]

Saved from Sin, Slaved by Grace

God's gift of redemption brings salvation from both sin's oppression and sin's consequences—and one day from its very existence. Hence,

---

23. 1 Cor. 1:30; cf. Matt. 26:28.

24. Cf. Eph. 4:32; Col. 2:13. Though we are no longer under sin's power (Rom. 6:14–19), the reality is that, because the new creation is incarcerated in unredeemed human flesh, we will still struggle with sin in this life (Rom. 7:21–24; 1 John 1:8) until the full redemption of the body (Rom. 8:18–23). The redemptive work that Christ does at salvation never needs to be repeated—atonement and justification are complete at that point. Yet, all who have been cleansed by God's gracious justification need constant washing in the experiential sense as they battle sin in the flesh and grow in sanctification. As the Lord told Peter, "He who has bathed needs only to wash his feet, but is completely clean" (John 13:10). Thus, we are called on to regularly confess our sins (1 John 1:9), asking for the forgiveness of daily cleansing that restores spiritual intimacy and usefulness to their maximum levels (cf. Matt. 6:12, 14–15). By being quick to confess and turn from sin, believers can bask in the profound spiritual blessings of both the redemption from sin and fellowship with God they enjoy through Christ (1 John 1:3; cf. Heb. 10:19), while awaiting full redemption from sin's presence in glory.

we no longer need to fear our former master; neither should we fear the wrath of God.[25] Christ defeated sin and Satan at the cross, and He also bore the full punishment of God's wrath for all who believe in Him. His death has set us free from sin, condemnation, and fear.[26]

Yet, we must not think that our redemption has somehow given us a license to sin. In fact, just the opposite is true.[27] When we were slaves to sin, we were "free in regard to righteousness" (Rom. 6:20). But now that we have been bought with a price, we are "slaves of righteousness" (v. 18), "having been freed from sin and enslaved to God" (v. 22).[28] We have been set free *from sin*, which means we are now free to obey, to live righteously, and to pursue holiness. We are slaves of Christ, "but here is the wonderful and very striking thing: *To be a slave of Jesus Christ is true freedom.*"[29] Murray Harris has observed:

> One of the classic Christian paradoxes is that freedom leads to slavery and slavery leads to freedom. As soon as people are set free through Christ from slavery to sin, they enter a new, permanent slavery to Christ. Indeed, the one slavery is terminated precisely in order to allow the other slavery to begin. While that emancipation happens

---

25. Cf. 1 Cor. 15:56–57; 1 John 4:17–18.

26. Cf. John 8:34–36; Rom. 8:15, 33–34; Heb. 2:14–15.

27. Cf. Rom. 6:1–2, 15. F. Büchsel describes the Christlike ethic that accompanies the saving faith of the redeemed: "To accept the forgiveness of Jesus is to accept the gift of Him who in willing obedience made of His whole existence, of His life and death, an offering to God, so that those who accept this forgiveness are not left at rest until they render the same obedience to God" (s.v. "λυτρόω," in *Theological Dictionary of the New Testament* [unabridged], 4:348).

28. Commenting on Romans 6:18, Douglas Moo wrote, "The passive verb here (as in vv. 17 and 22) draws attention again to the initiative of God" (*The Wycliffe Exegetical Commentary, Romans 1–8* [Chicago: Moody Press, 1991], 419).

29. James Montgomery Boice, *Romans*, 4 vols. (Grand Rapids: Baker, 1991), 2:690.

individually, the persons who are freed are not simply isolated "slaves of Christ." They form a worldwide community of "fellow-slaves," all belonging to the one Master who purchased their freedom and all committed to obeying and pleasing him.[30]

Unlike sin, Christ is the perfect Master—a point we have already discussed in detail. But the contrast cannot be overstated, because it could not be any starker. Sin is the cruelest and most unjust of all masters; Christ is the most loving and merciful. Sin's burden is heavy and loathsome; Christ's "yoke is easy" and His "burden is light" (Matt. 11:30). Sin traps its slaves in darkness and death; Christ brings light and life to all those who have been "made . . . alive together with Him" (Col. 2:13). Sin diverts, deceives, and destroys; Christ is "the way, and the truth, and the life" (John 14:6). Insofar as slavery to sin consists of everything hateful, harmful, dreadful, and despicable, so slavery to Christ entails everything good, glorious, joyous, and right.

> To serve God "under grace" is a liberating experience, as different as can be from slavery to sin. And not only is there a great difference in character between the two forms of service; there is a great difference between the ends to which they lead. Sin pays wages to its servants, the wages being death. God does not pay his servants mere wages: he gives them something better and much more generous. In his grace he gives life eternal as a free gift—that life eternal which is theirs by union with Christ.[31]

---

30. Harris, *Slave of Christ*, 153.

31. F. F. Bruce, *Romans, Tyndale New Testament Commentary* (repr., Grand Rapids: Eerdmans, 2002), 133.

Freedom in Christ, then, is not freedom *to* sin but freedom *from* sin—freedom to live as God intends, in truth and holiness (cf. 1 Peter 1:16). "The freedom of the Christian is not freedom to do what he or she wants but freedom to obey God—willingly, joyfully, naturally."[32] After all, for believers, "sin will no more be their lord, because another lord has taken possession of them, namely, Christ."[33] As one commentator explains, "[F]reedom in Christ is not an invitation to splendid self-centeredness. The freed in Christ have become slaves to righteousness. They are not aimless, purposeless. They have been freed from sin in order that they may give themselves wholly to worthwhile causes. . . . Those set free do not wander in a moral vacuum. They are *slaves to righteousness*."[34] True freedom begins when slavery to sin ends, and slavery to sin ends only when we have become the slaves of God. But as we will see in the following chapters, we are not just the slaves of God. We are also His citizens, friends, and family members. All of this is possible because He chose us and called us to Himself, redeeming us from our slavery to sin and granting us eternal life through His Son.

In chapter 7, we looked at the life and theology of John Newton—a man who understood both the terrors of enslavement to sin and the joys of wholehearted obedience to Christ. As we noted, Newton's grasp of this profound truth is reflected in the many hymns he wrote.

---

32. Moo, *The Wycliffe Exegetical Commentary, Romans 1–8*, 415. Moo added, "One is never free from a master, and those non-Christians who think they are free are under an illusion created and sustained by Satan. The choice with which people are faced is not, 'Should I retain my freedom, or give it up and submit to God?' but 'Should I serve sin, or should I serve God?'"

33. C. E. B. Cranfield, *The Epistle to the Romans*, 2 vols. (Edinburgh: T&T Clark, 1975), 1:319. On page 321, the author observes that Paul's use of the slavery metaphor "does express the total belongingness, total obligation and total accountability which characterize the life under grace, with a vigour and vividness which no other image seems able to equal."

34. Leon Morris, *The Epistle to the Romans, Pillar New Testament Commentary* (Grand Rapids: Eerdmans, 1998), 264.

Another famous hymn writer, a contemporary of Newton, is Charles Wesley. A prolific poet, Wesley wrote more than six thousand hymns, many of which we still sing today. The fourth verse of one of his best-known hymns, "And Can It Be," summarizes the glorious reality of God's redemption from sin, along with the believer's subsequent duty to follow and obey his new Master.

> *Long my imprisoned spirit lay,*
> *Fast bound in sin and nature's night;*
> *Thine eye diffused a quickening ray—*
> *I woke, the dungeon flamed with light;*
> *My chains fell off, my heart was free,*
> *I rose, went forth, and followed Thee.*

The hymn concludes with the resounding truth of the glorious hope that all the redeemed share in Christ.

> *No condemnation now I dread;*
> *Jesus, and all in Him, is mine;*
> *Alive in Him, my living Head,*
> *And clothed in righteousness divine,*
> *Bold I approach the eternal throne,*
> *And claim the crown, through Christ my own.*

ten

From Slaves to Sons (Part 1)

We have already discussed the doctrines of grace in some detail and noted the way in which Scripture uses slave language to illustrate those glorious themes. The doctrine of *total depravity* is seen in the fact that unbelievers are slaves to sin. They are both unwilling and unable to free themselves from sin's mastery over every area of their lives. Unless God intervenes, they are hopeless and helpless captives to sin, under the domain of darkness and headed for eternal destruction.

The doctrine of *sovereign election* teaches that God, in His infinite mercy, chose to save those sinners on whom He had set His love in eternity past. Even when we were at enmity with Him, God pursued us—drawing us to Himself by means of His *irresistible grace*. He rescued us from sin, transformed our hearts, and transferred us into the kingdom of His Son. Though we were once slaves to sin, we are now slaves to Christ and slaves to righteousness. A slave in Roman times did not choose his master. Rather, the master always chose the slave. Left to our own fallen reasoning, you and I would have never chosen God. But according to His great mercy, He chose us—initiating and accomplishing everything necessary for our salvation.

The doctrine of *particular redemption* is also brought out by the marketplace language of Scripture, where a business transaction or ransom is pictured. Christ's death on the cross actually pays the penalty for the elect sinner, redeeming him from sin and rescuing him from God's wrath. In Roman times, the master paid only for the slaves he was purchasing. So also, the saving benefits of Christ's redemptive work are applied only to those whom God has chosen for Himself. Having been bought with a price, the precious blood of Christ, believers are His own possession.

In all of this, we as believers can take no credit. We were wholly in bondage to sin when God intervened by His own sovereign will and rescued us on the basis of Christ's redeeming work. Not only did God save us from sin, but He promises to keep us as His own—completing the work He began in us at conversion until it culminates in glorification.[1] This protective promise of God for His people, known as the *perseverance of the saints* (or also *the eternal security of the believer*), guarantees that those whom He chose in eternity past will be saved in the present and glorified in the future. As Paul outlined the process in Romans 8:30, "these whom He predestined, He also called; and these whom He called, He also justified; and these whom He justified, He also glorified." The slaves whom He has rescued from sin and purchased for Himself will remain in His household forever.

It is this last point, our permanent placement in the household of God, which we will examine in the upcoming pages. As we have already seen, when God rescues unbelievers from sin, He makes them His own slaves. Yet, He does not stop there. In salvation, the redeemed become not only His slaves but also His friends (John 15:14–15), as well as citizens in His kingdom and, most notably, adopted children in His family. Believers have been transformed from slaves of sin into the

---

1. John 6:39; 10:27–29; Phil. 1:6; Rom. 8:38–39.

sons and daughters of righteousness. As fourth-century church father John Chrysostom marveled many centuries ago:

> First there is the freeing from sin, and then there is the making of slaves of righteousness, which is better than any freedom. For God has done the same as if a person was to take an orphan who had been carried away by savages into their own country, and was not only to free him from captivity but to set a kind of father over him and raise him to a very great dignity. This is what has happened in our case. For it was not just that God freed us from our old evils; He also led us into the life of angels. He opened the way for us to enjoy the best life, handing us over to the safekeeping of righteousness and killing our former evils, putting the old man in us to death and bringing us to eternal life.[2]

A Father to the Fatherless

George Müller was around thirty years old when he and his wife, Mary, began their ministry to the orphans in Bristol, England. George had begun pastoring in Bristol several years earlier (in 1832), and now he and Mary opened their own home to needy children. As biographer Arthur T. Pierson explained, Müller's "loving heart had been drawn out toward poverty and misery everywhere, but especially in the case of destitute children bereft of both parents."[3]

The work that began with an initial thirty orphans quickly expanded.

---

2. John Chrysostom, *Homilies on Romans*, 11, quoted in Gerald Bray, ed., *Romans, Ancient Christian Commentary on Scripture* (Downers Grove, IL: InterVarsity, 1998), 170.

3. Arthur Tappan Pierson, *George Müller of Bristol* (London: James Nisbet & Co., 1899), 116.

Other homes were furnished, and an additional one hundred orphans were admitted. But the need was greater still. So in 1849, a separate building was constructed that could hold three hundred orphans. By 1870, there were five large buildings, housing a total of two thousand children. In a day when orphans comprised close to 60 percent of England's criminal population,[4] Müller's ministry saved thousands of young people from life on the streets and in prison. But more important, his evangelistic emphasis meant that many of these same children believed the gospel and were saved from sin and its eternal consequences. As his biographer explained, Müller's "main hope was to be the means of spiritual health to these children." Nonetheless, "he had the joy of seeing how God used these homes for the promotion of their physical welfare also, and, in cases not a few, for the entire renovation of their weak and diseased bodies."[5]

In this work, George Müller was motivated not only out of compassion for destitute children but also out of a deep-seated conviction that was rooted in the doctrines of grace. He was in his mid-twenties when he began to seriously examine those profound biblical realities—including the total depravity of man and the sovereign election of God in salvation. At first, he adamantly rejected them. As he would later recount, "Before this period I had been much opposed to the doctrines of election, particular redemption, and final persevering grace; so much so that . . . I called election a devilish doctrine."[6]

---

4. Based on the reports of E. C. Tufnell, the inspector of parochial union schools in 1853–54, cited in Laura Peters, *Orphan Texts* (New York: Manchester University Press, 2000), 9.

5. Pierson, *George Müller of Bristol*, 226.

6. George Müller, *A Narrative of Some of the Lord's Dealing with George Müller, Written by Himself, Jehovah Magnified. Addresses by George Müller Complete and Unabridged*, 2 vols. (Muskegon, MI: Dust and Ashes, 2003), 1:46.

But as the young Müller began to examine the Scriptures, his understanding dramatically changed. What had previously seemed to him as "devilish doctrine[s]" soon became precious truths:

> I went to the Word, reading the New Testament from the beginning, with a particular reference to these truths. To my great astonishment I found that the passages which speak decidedly for election and persevering grace, were about four times as many as those which speak apparently against these truths; and even those few, shortly after, when I had examined and understood them, served to confirm me in the above doctrines.[7]

In this way, George Müller came to believe "that the Father chose us before the foundation of the world, . . . that he also appointed all the means by which [our redemption] was to be brought about, . . . that the Son, to save us, had fulfilled the law [and] had borne the punishment due to our sins, . . . [and] that the Holy Spirit alone can teach us about our state by nature, show us the need of a Saviour, [and] enable us to believe in Christ."[8] Having thoroughly investigated God's Word, He now wholeheartedly embraced the doctrines of total depravity, sovereign election, irresistible grace, particular redemption, and the perseverance of the saints.

Much of Müller's initial opposition to these doctrines stemmed from his misconception that they would dampen his evangelistic zeal. To his surprise, and great joy, they had exactly the opposite effect. As a result, he could say:

---

7. Ibid., 1:46.

8. George Müller, *The Life of Trust* (New York: Thomas Y. Crowell, 1898), 70.

In the course of time . . . it pleased God then to show to me the doctrines of grace in a way in which I had not seen them before. At first I hated them, "If this were true I could do nothing at all in the conversion of sinners, as all would depend upon God and the working of His Spirit." But when it pleased God to reveal these truths to me, and my heart was brought to such a state that I could say, "I am not only content simply to be a hammer, an axe, or a saw, in God's hands; but I shall count it an honor to be taken up and used by Him in any way; and if sinners are converted through my instrumentality, from my inmost soul I will give Him all the glory;" the Lord gave me to see fruit; the Lord gave me to see fruit in abundance; sinners were converted by scores; and ever since God has used me in one way or other in His service.[9]

Müller's understanding of these biblical and reformational doctrines further served to strengthen his personal walk with God. Reflecting on his own progressive sanctification, he noted:

As to the effect which my belief in these doctrines had on me, I am constrained to state, for God's glory, that though I am still exceedingly weak, and by no means so dead to the lusts of the flesh, and the lust of the eyes, and the pride of life, as I might and as I ought to be, yet, by the grace of God, I have walked more closely with Him since that period. My life has not been so variable, and I may say that I have lived much more for God than before.[10]

---

9. Müller, *Narrative*, 1:752.

10. Ibid., 1:46.

Fueled by a new understanding of God's grace in salvation, George Müller embarked on a path of profound and sacrificial ministry. Over the course of his lifetime, he would oversee the care of one hundred thousand orphans in nineteenth-century England—providing for them and educating them to the point that he was accused of elevating poor children above their natural station in life. As a fervent prayer warrior, he never solicited funds for his orphan houses but rather took all of his requests directly to the Lord. As an itinerant evangelist, a work he began in earnest at age seventy, he traveled more than 200,000 arduous and slow miles, preaching in the United States, Australia, India, China, Japan, and dozens of other countries. In all of this, Müller's heart was captivated by an indefatigable desire to serve and glorify his Lord. Having been rescued from slavery to sin, he was now the willing slave of Jesus Christ. As D. Martyn Lloyd-Jones observed,

> A statement which the great George Müller once made about himself seems to illustrate this very clearly. He writes like this: "There was a day when I died, utterly died, died to George Müller and his opinions, preferences, tastes and will; died to the world, its approval or censure; died to the approval or blame of even my brethren and friends; and since then I have studied only to show myself approved unto God." That is a statement to be pondered deeply.[11]

Of this tireless laborer for the sake of the gospel, "it was touchingly remarked at [Müller's] funeral that he first confessed to feeling weak and weary in his work that last night of his earthly sojourn."[12] The

---

11. D. Martyn Lloyd-Jones, *Studies in the Sermon on the Mount*, 2 volumes in 1 (Grand Rapids: Eerdmans, 1976), 1:257.

12. Pierson, *George Müller of Bristol*, 290.

next morning, sometime before seven o'clock, God took him home to heaven. His last sermon, preached several months earlier, had appropriately been focused on the hope of future resurrection. His text was 2 Corinthians 5:1, "For we know that if the earthly tent which is our house is torn down, we have a building from God, a house not made with hands, eternal in the heavens." Armed with the certainty of that hope and confident in God's sovereign grace, George Müller entered his eternal rest on March 10, 1898.

From a theological perspective, George Müller is noteworthy, not only for his commitment to the doctrines of grace but also for the way those doctrines motivated him to pray, evangelize, and care for others. He understood that he was a slave of Christ. And he was faithful to live that out.

But Müller's ministry also serves, in a small way, as an illustration of another great spiritual reality. His compassion for destitute children pictures the kindness and love that God showers on those whom He saves. The children whom Müller rescued from the streets of England had no provision, no protection, and no future beyond a life of hardship and crime. Yet he brought them under his care and became to them a second father—even though they could offer nothing in return. So also, God rescues sinners from the oppression and misery of sin. He exchanges their filthy rags for robes of righteousness, welcomes them into His house, invites them to sit at His table, and promises them a glorious future.

From Slaves to Sons

That God, in His grace, would free us from sin and make us His slaves is a wondrous truth to comprehend. What a privilege it is for us to know and obey the heavenly Master! As we noted in chapter 6, a slave's dignity was derived from the power and position of his owner. In ancient times, the slaves of the king were the most highly respected of all. We belong to the King of kings—God Himself. There can be no higher honor than that. And yet the Lord has bestowed an even greater distinction upon those who are His own.

Having delivered us from the destitution of sin, God not only receives us as His slaves—but He has also welcomed us into His household and made us members of His very family. He not only rescued us, purchased us, befriended us, and took us in; He has also adopted us, thereby transforming those who were formerly children of wrath (Eph. 2:3) into the sons and daughters of righteousness. All of this is possible through the redemptive work of Christ, who is the "only begotten Son" (John 3:16), and the "firstborn among many brethren" (Rom. 8:29; cf. Rev. 1:5).[13]

The very term *adoption* is filled with ideas of compassion, kindness, grace, and love. But to fully understand the nuances of the New Testament metaphor, it is helpful to again turn our attention to ancient Rome.[14] Though the formal adoption of slaves was somewhat uncommon, it was permissible under Roman law[15] and did occur in certain

---

13. The term *firstborn*, when applied to Jesus Christ, does not imply that He was created (as some cult groups claim). Rather, in both Jewish and Greco-Roman culture, the "firstborn" was the ranking son who was given the right of inheritance, whether he was born first or not. Thus, the title "firstborn" means "highest ranking" or "preeminent."

14. For a discussion as to why Roman, rather than Greek, law is behind much of the New Testament's adoption language, see Francis Lyall, *Slaves, Citizens, Sons: Legal Metaphors in the Epistles* (Grand Rapids: Academie Books, 1984), 95–99.

15. Cf. Lyall, *Slaves, Citizens, Sons*, 125–26. Though adoption, in general, was fairly common, the formal adoption of slaves, in particular, was much rarer. Informally, any manumitted slave would view his former master—namely, the one who set him free—as a father figure or *patron* (cf. James S. Jeffers, *The Greco-Roman World of the New Testament* [Downers Grove, IL: InterVarsity Press, 1999], 239). Because God set us free from slavery to sin, this analogy

instances.[16] The extraordinary nature of the practice makes God's adoptive love toward us all the more remarkable—in that He has done the unexpected by adopting all His slaves as His own children[17] and naming us His heirs (Rom. 8:17). In ancient Rome, the act of adoption immediately granted the former slave his freedom, permanently placing him into the family of his master.[18] So also, as the adopted children of God, we have been set free from slavery to sin. Moreover, we can rest assured in knowing that we have been given a permanent place in the family of God.

Adoption, in Roman times, signified a new beginning: entrance into a new family such that all previous family ties and obligations were broken. The adoption process consisted of several specific legal procedures. The first step completely terminated the adopted child's social relationship and legal connection to his natural family. The second step made him a permanent member of his new family.[19] Additionally, any previous financial obligations were eradicated, as if they had never

---

could also apply to the believer. However, the New Testament language of adoption assumes the formal legal process, in which the full privileges of sonship and an inheritance are officially bestowed.

16. Cf. William W. Buckland, *A Text-Book of Roman Law* (Cambridge, UK: Cambridge University Press, 1963), 127–28. Brian J. Dodd, in *The Problem with Paul* (Downers Grove, IL: InterVarsity, 1996), gives an example of a Macedonian boy named Vitalis who was born into slavery but was later freed and adopted by his owner (97).

17. The New Testament refers to believers as the children of God on numerous occasions (e.g., Gal. 3:16, 26, 29; Eph. 5:1, 8; Phil. 2:15; 1 Thess. 5:5; Heb. 2:10; 12:5–11; 1 John 3:1–3).

18. Thus we read, in the introduction to *The Institutes of Gaius and Justinian*, "The adoption of slaves by their masters gives them their freedom" (T. Lambert Mears [Clark, NJ: Lawbook Exchange, 2005], xxxvii).

19. Francis Lyall explains that "there were two stages in the *adoptio* procedure. The first was the destruction of the old *potestas*, the paternal power of the 'previous' father. The second stage was the establishing of the paternal power of the 'new' father. . . . Thereafter the adoptee was subject to the authority and direction of his new paterfamilias in all matters" (*Slaves, Citizens, Sons*, 86–87).

existed.[20] In order for the transaction to be legally formalized, the presence of seven reputable witnesses was required. If necessary, their testimony would refute any potential challenge to the adoption after the father had died.[21]

Once the adoption was complete, the new son or daughter was then completely under both the care and control of the new father. The previous father no longer had any authority over his former child. In Roman households, the authority of the *paterfamilias* ("father of the family") was final and absolute. And that authority extended to those adopted into the household, starting at the moment of their adoption. As one scholar explains, "From that time on the paterfamilias had the same control over his new 'child' as he had over his natural offspring. He owned all the property and acquisitions of the adoptee, controlled his personal relationships, and had rights of discipline."[22]

Such imagery certainly undergirds the New Testament instruction regarding how "one ought to conduct himself in the household of God" (1 Tim. 3:15).[23] It also explains biblical allusions to God's fatherly discipline, "for what son is there whom his father does not discipline?" (Heb. 12:7).

But unlike earthly fathers, who are sometimes prone to anger and harshness, God is a perfect Father. Moreover, because of our position

---

20. Cf. Everett Ferguson, *Backgrounds of Early Christianity* (Grand Rapids: Eerdmans, 2003), 65–66.

21. Though Roman adoptions were primarily intended to benefit the new father (by providing him with a suitable heir), the New Testament's focus is on how adoption benefits believers— underscoring the marvelous nature of God's gracious provision (cf. James C. Walters, "Paul, Adoption, and Inheritance," pp. 42–76 in *Paul in the Greco-Roman World*, ed. J. Paul Sampley [Harrisburg, PA: Trinity Press, 2003], 58).

22. Lyall, *Slaves, Citizens, Sons*, 83.

23. Cf. Gal. 6:10; Eph. 2:19–22; 1 Peter 4:17.

in Christ, God now views us and treats us as He does His own Son—with infinite love.[24] The Father cannot give anything but His best to His Son. Likewise, He will not give anything but His best to those of us who are in Christ—which is why we can "know that God causes all things to work together for good to those who love God, to those who are called according to His purpose" (Rom. 8:28). One scholar explains: "While the distinction between Jesus as the unique Son of God and believers as sons and daughters of God in Christ is not obliterated (e.g., John 20:17), believers nevertheless become in a real, spiritual sense brothers and sisters of Jesus as well as of one another."[25] The author of Hebrews says it this way: "Both He who sanctifies and those who are sanctified are all from one Father; for which reason He is not ashamed to call them brethren" (2:11). And later, "Christ was faithful as a Son over His house—whose house we are, if we hold fast our confidence and the boast of our hope firm until the end" (3:6).

Paul was well aware of Roman adoption customs and likely had them in mind when he used the language of adoption in his epistles. In Galatians 4 he emphasized that those who were previously slaves to Judaistic legalism had now been freed through the adoption of grace:

> But when the fullness of the time came, God sent forth His Son . . . so that He might redeem those who were under the Law, that we might receive the adoption as sons. Because you are sons, God has sent

---

24. As J. I. Packer explains, "The adopted status of believers means that in and through Christ God loves them as he loves his only-begotten Son and will share with them all the glory that is Christ's now" (*Concise Theology* [Wheaton, IL: Tyndale House, 1993], 167).

25. Andreas J. Kostenberger with David W. Jones, *God, Marriage, and Family* (Wheaton, IL: Crossway, 2004), 150. The point is further explained by Walter Elwell: "Adoption makes it clear that our sonship is conferred on us, in distinction from Christ's, which is inherent" (*The Shaw Pocket Bible Handbook* [Wheaton, IL: Harold Shaw, 1984], 346).

forth the Spirit of His Son into our hearts, crying, "Abba! Father!" Therefore you are no longer a slave [to the legalism of the Mosaic Law], but a son; and if a son, then an heir through God." (vv. 4–7)

In Romans 8:14–17, the apostle made a similar point—this time emphasizing that adoption frees us from slavery to sin and the fear of death:[26]

For all who are being led by the Spirit of God, these are sons of God. For you have not received a spirit of slavery [to sin] leading to fear again, but you have received a spirit of adoption as sons by which we cry out, "Abba! Father!" The Spirit Himself testifies with our spirit that we are children of God, and if children, heirs also, heirs of God and fellow heirs with Christ, if indeed we suffer with Him so that we may also be glorified with Him.

These two passages underscore important truths about the believer's adoption into the family of God. Though we were formerly enslaved to sin and the condemnation of the Law, we have been permanently liberated through our adoption into the family of God. As His adopted children, we enjoy the profound privilege of an intimate relationship with our heavenly Father, to whom we cry out with child-like affection, "Abba!"

A term of intimate endearment, *Abba* is an informal Aramaic term for "Father." It expresses tenderness, dependence, and a childlike assurance that lacks any anxiety or fear. Jesus Himself used the term in the

---

26. As John Byron has noted, "The notion of adoption in [Romans] 8.15 is not made to contrast with slavery as such, but with a particular type of slavery, i.e. to sin" (*Slavery Metaphors in Early Judaism and Pauline Christianity* [Tubingen, Germany: J. C. B. Mohr, 2003], 228).

Garden of Gethsemane when He poured out His heart to His Father (Mark 14:36). That we would be allowed to address the Father in the same way Jesus did underscores the magnificent reality of our adoption. To be considered "heirs of God and fellow heirs with Christ" is a remarkable truth, and one that we should never take for granted.

To think that we, who were once the slaves of sin, the subjects of Satan, and the sons of disobedience, are now and forever the slaves of Christ, the citizens of heaven, and the children of God—such is the joy and wonder of salvation. As His enemies, we did not even deserve to be His slaves. Yet, He has made us both His slaves and His children. The incomparable reality of adoption is this: If God is our Master, then He is also our Father. As Alexander Maclaren, the great Scottish preacher, explained, "If we are slaves, then we are sons and heirs of God through Jesus Christ."[27]

---

27. Alexander Maclaren, *Expositions of Holy Scripture, the Acts* (n.p.: Bibliolife, 2007), 149.

eleven

From Slaves to Sons (Part 2)

Within the last two decades, a myriad of new books have documented the joy and wonder of adoption.[1] Even a quick read through the personal experiences of both adoptive parents and adopted children is enough to warm the heart. In story after story, orphans trapped in desperate circumstances are rescued by people who deeply care about them, even though they had never previously met. Would-be parents, eager to show love and compassion to a helpless child, fill out hundreds of forms and travel thousands of miles to make their families complete. Though the process takes months, everything changes for the child in a moment—when the judge finally declares him to be the legal heir of his adoptive parents. Had the child been left in the orphanage or in the care of abusive and neglectful birth parents, the outcome would likely have been tragic. But now, through the intervention of those who were formerly strangers, a little boy or girl is given a brand-new home filled with the love of a family and the hope of a future. Such is the miracle of adoption.

The New Testament builds on the joy and wonder of human adoption by using it as an analogy to describe God's fatherly love for us. We were spiritual orphans, under the cruel oppression of sin and Satan. As Scripture depicts it, we were "children of wrath" (Eph. 2:3), "sons

---

1. A recommended resource in this regard is Russell D. Moore's *Adopted for Life* (Wheaton, IL: Crossway, 2009).

of disobedience" (Eph. 2:2; 5:6), "slaves of sin" (Rom. 6:17), and the followers of our "father the devil" (John 8:44). We had no home but this world, no guardian but Satan, and no future but hell. Had we been left in that condition, we would have died in our sins and perished eternally. "But God, being rich in mercy, because of His great love with which He loved us, even when we were dead in our transgressions, made us alive together with Christ (by grace you have been saved)" (Eph. 2:4–5). At great cost to Himself, God intervened to rescue us from sin and bring us into fellowship with Him. In that moment, the Judge of the universe declared us righteous, having clothed us in the sinless perfection of Jesus Christ.[2] He made us His slaves, brought us into His kingdom, and welcomed us into His family. Such is the miracle of our spiritual adoption.

Adoption and the Old Testament

As we saw in the previous chapter, the New Testament doctrine of adoption begins to come alive when we understand the legal proceedings of first-century Rome. But, as with the slavery metaphor, we must also consider the history of ancient Israel, recognizing the theological backdrop that the Old Testament provides for the New Testament. In so doing, we will discover a profound richness that is added to our understanding of the biblical imagery.

One of the first adoptions recorded in the Old Testament was that

---

2. In the New Testament, there is a close connection between justification (the declaration of our righteousness in Christ) and adoption (our being placed into the family of God). As J. I. Packer has explained, "Justification is the basic blessing, on which adoption is founded; adoption is the crowning blessing, to which justification clears the way" (*Concise Theology* [Wheaton, IL: Tyndale House, 1993], 167).

of Moses,[3] whose life was spared when his mother floated him down the Nile River in a waterproof basket. When Pharaoh's daughter came to the river and found him, she took pity on him. Miriam—Moses' sister, who had been watching from nearby—offered to find a suitable nursemaid for the baby, and Pharaoh's daughter agreed. As a result, Moses was returned to his birth mother until he was old enough to go live in the palace. At that time, he was brought to "Pharaoh's daughter and he became her son" (Ex. 2:10). Thus, Moses—the son of slaves—became part of the royal family of Egypt (cf. Acts 7:20–21).

Esther is another notable Old Testament example of adoption. When her parents died, she was taken in by Mordecai, her older cousin. He cared for her as a father, making sure to look after her welfare (cf. Esth. 2:5–11). Even after she became queen, Esther continued to look to Mordecai for parental guidance and encouragement.

One of the most heart-warming accounts in the Old Testament is that of Mephibosheth, who for all practical purposes was adopted by King David.[4] Mephibosheth was the crippled son of Jonathan, David's closest friend, and sole surviving descendant of King Saul. After learning about Mephibosheth, David invited him to dine regularly at his own royal table. He also gave him the land that had previously belonged to his grandfather Saul (2 Sam. 9:1–13).

Because David's adoption of Mephibosheth was motivated by

---

3. Before Moses, Abraham made Eliezer his heir (Gen. 15:2), which some commentators believe included some type of adoption. Abraham may have also adopted his nephew Lot (according to Josephus, *Antiquities*, I.7.1). Similarly, Jacob adopted Ephraim and Manasseh, his grandsons through Joseph (Gen. 48:5). In so doing, he made them the fathers of two of the tribes of Israel.

4. Though formal adoption, in the sense of a legal institution, did not exist among the ancient Hebrews, the Old Testament includes several "instances of *essential*, though *not formal* or *technical, adoption*" (William Hendrickson, *Romans, New Testament Commentary* [Grand Rapids: Baker, 1981], 259). In this sense, Mephibosheth was adopted by David.

nothing more than gracious love, his actions give us a wonderful glimpse into God's adoptive love for believers. For instance, David took all of the initiative. He sought out Mephibosheth and welcomed him to the palace. He did so even though Mephibosheth was the grandson and heir of Saul—Israel's previous king and David's greatest persecutor. As a cripple, Mephibosheth could do nothing to repay David or offer him any significant service. Even Mephibosheth's name, which means "a shameful thing," underscores the fact that he was an outcast. But David brought him into his family, invited him to his table, and even granted him an inheritance of land to which he was not legally entitled.

What a magnificent picture of our spiritual adoption by God. We were not seeking Him, yet He found us and saved us. We were His enemies, yet He made us His friends. We could offer Him nothing in return, yet He bestowed on us an inheritance we did not deserve. All of this is ours by grace through faith in His only begotten Son, Jesus Christ. To all believers God declares, "I will welcome you. And I will be a father to you, and you shall be sons and daughters to Me" (2 Cor. 6:17–18).

The apostle Paul would have been familiar with each of these Old Testament accounts. He would also have been aware that the adoption of slaves, in particular, occurred not only in Rome but in ancient Jewish society as well.[5] In such circumstances

> an adopted slave was always considered a real member of the family, and his name was registered as such, not only in the family register, but with the other members of the family, in the archives of the city;

---

5. Cf. Catherine Hezser, *Jewish Slavery in Antiquity* (Oxford University Press, 2005), 138–39.

and the book in which it was so registered was called in Jerusalem "Book of Life," or the "Book of the Living." So the names of all the Lord's adopted ones are registered in the Book of Life of the Heavenly Jerusalem; and the beauty of this is it is also the *King's* family, not a beggar's, into which he is registered; and he is as welcome at the table as the king himself.[6]

Significantly, the adoption of slaves was illustrated, corporately, by the nation of Israel itself. In the Exodus, this nation was liberated from bondage in Egypt and adopted by God. As an expert in the Old Testament, Paul would have readily drawn on passages such as Exodus 4:22, Deuteronomy 14:1–2; 32:5–6; and Hosea 1:10; 11:1—texts that describe the Israelites as God's adopted children.[7] Paul understood that just as "Israel was released from the control of Pharaoh to serve God; the believer was released from the control of sin to serve God. Both are declared by God to be [His] sons."[8] In the same way that Israel was adopted by God (Rom. 9:4), New Testament Christians have been welcomed as children into His family.[9]

Due to his Roman citizenship and his rabbinical training, it is not

---

6. John Gadsby, *Slavery, Adoption, and Redemption* (n.p.: Primitive Baptist Publishing House, 1865), 34.

7. Cf. James M. Scott, *Adoption as Sons of God* (Tubingen, Germany: J. C. B. Mohr, 1992). Sometimes 2 Samuel 7:14 is interpreted this way as well.

8. John Byron, *Slavery Metaphors in Early Judaism and Pauline Christianity* (Tubingen, Germany: J. C. B. Mohr, 2003), 228.

9. Along these lines, Russell D. Moore has written, "Too often we assume that the Gentiles are the 'adopted' children of God, and the Jews are the 'natural-born' children. But Paul says that Israel was adopted too (Rom. 9:4). Of Israel, God once said, 'Your origin and your birth are of the land of the Canaanites; your father was an Amorite and your mother a Hittite' (Ezek. 16:3). The Israelites were once Gentiles too. God reminds Israel that he 'found him in a desert land, and in the howling waste of the wilderness' (Deut. 32:10). Israel was an abandoned baby, wallowing in its own blood on the roadside (Ezek. 16:5)" (*Adopted for Life*, 30).

surprising that Paul drew his adoption imagery from both Roman and Jewish adoption practices.[10] All of it underscores the richness of the adoption metaphor—especially in light of the believer's former status as an enemy of God and a slave to sin. Could there be any greater honor or privilege than to be an adopted child of God? "Adoption brings us all the benefits of sonship, including the right to approach God in prayer. It assures us of God's love and protection. It contributes to our assurance that we have been saved."[11] It is no wonder that Paul exclaimed in Ephesians 1:3–5, "Blessed be the God and Father of our Lord Jesus Christ, who has blessed us with every spiritual blessing in the heavenly places in Christ, just as He chose us in Him before the foundation of the world, that we should be holy and blameless before Him. In love He predestined us to adoption as sons through Jesus Christ to Himself, according to the kind intention of His will.

In eternity past, God graciously and sovereignly chose every believer to be part of His family forever! As "heirs according to the hope of eternal life" (Titus 3:7), we will spend all of eternity in joyous worship and intimate fellowship with the God who saved us. As David exulted in Psalm 16:5, "The LORD is the portion of my inheritance and

---

10. William Hendrickson has explained these dual influences on Paul's use of the adoption metaphor in this way: "When in Rom. 8:15 and Gal. 4:5 Paul uses the term 'adoption' the *word* and the *legal standing* were borrowed from Roman practice, but the *essence* from the divine revelation in the Old Testament" (*Romans* [Grand Rapids: Baker, 1991], 259. Cf. Douglas J. Moo, *The Epistle of Romans, New International Commentary on the New Testament* [Grand Rapids: Eerdmans, 1996], 501), hereafter referred to as *NICNT*. Though commentators disagree on which was more prominent in Paul's mind (Roman adoption or Jewish adoption), the two are not mutually exclusive—and it is likely that Paul (as both a Roman citizen and a trained rabbi) drew his imagery from both worlds. As Rupert Davies stated, "Both Jewish and Roman customs are no doubt in mind" (*The Westminster Dictionary of Christian Theology*, ed. Alan Richardson and John Bowden [Philadelphia: Westminster Press, 1983], s.v. "Adoption," 5).

11. James M. Boice and Philip G. Ryken, *The Doctrines of Grace* (Wheaton, IL: Crossway, 2003), 151–52.

my cup." Our incredible future will also include a particularly amazing aspect of our adoption—the resurrection of our bodies in a glorified state that is free from sin. Paul noted this in Romans 8:23 when he wrote, "We ourselves groan within ourselves, waiting eagerly for our adoption as sons, the redemption of our body."[12]

In his vision recorded in the book of Revelation, the apostle John "heard a loud voice from the throne, saying, 'Behold, the tabernacle of God is among men, and He will dwell among them, and they shall be His people, and God Himself will be among them, and He will wipe away every tear from their eyes; and there will no longer be any death; there will no longer be any mourning, or crying, or pain. . . . He who overcomes will inherit these things, and I will be his God and he will be My son" (21:3–4, 7). What a glorious promise that is!

In the Family Forever

One of the most reassuring aspects of the doctrine of adoption is that it speaks of a permanent relationship. In this way, the biblical doctrine of adoption "is analogous to the act of a modern court by which a husband and wife become adoptive parents of children who are not their natural offspring."[13] Whether we are discussing modern-day adoptions

---

12. Commenting on this verse, Thomas R. Schreiner and Ardel B. Caneday noted, "As Christians we are adopted into God's family, yet we will not experience the consummation of our adoption until the day of the resurrection" (*The Race Set Before Us* [Downers Grove, IL: InterVarsity, 2001], 68). This is partly why Paul uses the image of "inheritance," since it emphasizes the future implications of a present reality (cf. Douglas Moo, *The Epistle to the Romans*, NICNT, 504).

13. Norman Shepherd, "Adoption" in the *Baker Encyclopedia of the Bible*, eds. W. A. Elwell and B. J. Beitzel (Grand Rapids: Baker, 1988), I:31.

or the biblical doctrine of adoption, the change in status is always a permanent one.[14]

Whereas a master/slave relationship might be temporary, a father/ son relationship is not. As Jesus told the unbelieving Pharisees, under-scoring the axiomatic nature of this reality, "The slave does not remain in the house forever; the son does remain forever" (John 8:35). In con-text, Jesus was warning the Pharisees (who thought they were God's children through Abraham) that they were, in reality, the slaves of sin (v. 34), in desperate need of liberation through the Son of God (v. 36). As is true for all who are sin's slaves, their future was transitory and bleak. Only through faith in Christ could they be freed from sin. And once freed, they would be adopted into the true family of God—trad-ing something that was temporary for an *eternal* position.

The doctrine of adoption establishes the reality that believers, once saved, are always saved. As one scholar, commenting on Paul's use of adoption imagery, has explained, "The important term 'adoption' bears a relationship to justification in that it is declarative and forensic (inasmuch as it is a legal term). Adoption bestows an objective stand-ing, as justification does: like justification, it is a pronouncement that is not repeated. *It has permanent validity.* Like justification, adoption rests on the loving purpose and grace of God."[15]

Well-known British preacher D. Martyn Lloyd-Jones made the

---

14. In our own day, and even at the most basic level, adoption is widely understood as a permanent arrangement. As one secular writer has expressed it, "Adoption is a *permanent* option. An adopted child has the same legal rights and privileges as a biological child. Adoption is not the same as *foster care* or *guardianship*, both of which are usually temporary (or are supposed to be). Instead, adoption is forever. In fact, many adoptive families refer to themselves as 'forever families'" (Christine A. Adamec, *The Complete Idiot's Guide to Adoption* [Indianapolis: Alpha Books, 1998], 7).

15. Everett F. Harrison, *Romans, Expositor's Bible Commentary* (Grand Rapids: Zondervan, 1996), 93. Emphasis added.

same point when he wrote, "If God has adopted you into His family, if you are a child of God, your destiny is secure, it is certain. . . . It is a guarantee. If God has taken me into the family I am not only a child, I am an heir, and nothing, and no one can ever rob me of the inheritance."[16]

If our adoption were not permanent, we would have great reason to fear. Our sin might yet condemn us. But "contrasted with this inner sense of dread before God, the righteous judge, is the sense of peace and security before God, our heavenly Father, that is produced by God's Spirit in the heart of Christians. Paul could hardly have chosen a better term than 'adoption' to characterize this peace and security."[17] Thus Paul's point in Romans 8:15 is that the *spirit of adoption* casts out the *spirit of fear* that comes from slavery to sin.[18] The Holy Spirit testifies to our spirits that we are the children of God (v. 16), and if we have the Holy Spirit, we have God's unbreakable seal guaranteeing our future inheritance.[19] Moreover, "adoption does not depend on any worthiness in us, but upon unmerited favor. It is all of grace."[20] We did nothing to earn our adoption into God's family, and we can do nothing to lose it either.

Later in Romans 8, Paul further underscored the permanence of our adoption. In verses 29–31, he explained that all those whom God has justified, He will glorify; none will be lost. In verses 32–34, he encouraged believers with the truth that no accusation made against God's elect will ever stick, because all has been forgiven through

16. D. Martyn Lloyd-Jones, *Great Doctrines of the Bible* (Wheaton, IL: Crossway, 2003), 189.

17. Moo, *The Epistle to the Romans*, NICNT, 500–1.

18. Cf. Heb. 2:14–15; 1 John 4:13, 18.

19. Cf. 2 Cor. 1:22; Eph. 1:13–14; 4:30.

20. Herbert Lockyer, *All the Doctrines of the Bible* (Grand Rapids: Zondervan, 1964), 203.

Christ. Finally, in verses 35–39, the apostle noted that there is absolutely nothing that can separate God's children from His eternal love. With our adoption complete, our security in God's family is forever fixed. The astonishing reality of adoption is that believers are given "a place in God's family just as eternal and secure as His only-begotten Son."[21]

The rest of the New Testament echoes the truth that believers, once saved, are always saved. This doctrine, known as the *eternal security of believers* or the *perseverance of the saints*, which I mentioned in the previous chapter, teaches that "all those who are truly born again will be kept by God's power and will persevere as Christians until the end of their lives, and that only those who persevere until the end have been truly born again."[22] In other words, a true believer can never lose his salvation. Once adopted into God's family, he becomes a child of God forever.[23] On the flip side, those who profess salvation but later fall away, demonstrate that their profession was never genuine (1 John 2:19).

The security of our salvation is asserted by numerous biblical texts. In John 6:39–40, Jesus promised that He would "lose nothing" of all that the Father has given Him, and that on the last day He will raise up "everyone who beholds the Son and believes in Him." In John 10:27–29, our Lord makes a similar declaration: "My sheep hear My

---

21. Kenneth S. Wuest, *Wuest's Word Studies from the Greek New Testament* (Grand Rapids: Eerdmans, 1997), 92.

22. Wayne Grudem, *Systematic Theology* (Grand Rapids: Zondervan, 1994), 788.

23. In the words of a nineteenth-century catechism based on Westminster, "How does their perseverance flow from *adoption*? A. In as much as he who has adopted them as his children, is their *everlasting Father*, Isa. ix. 6; and therefore they shall *abide* in his *house for ever*, John viii. 35" (*The Westminster Assembly's Shorter Catechism Explained* [Philadelphia: William S. Young, 1840], 199).

voice, and I know them, and they follow Me; and I give eternal life to them, and they will never perish; and no one will snatch them out of My hand. My Father, who has given them to Me, is greater than all; and no one is able to snatch them out of the Father's hand." Time and again, those who believe in Christ, turning from sin and wholeheartedly trusting in Him, are given the unqualified promise of eternal life.[24]

Believers can therefore be described as those for whom there remains "no condemnation" (Rom. 8:1). They have been sealed with the Holy Spirit, signifying the irrevocable nature of God's divine guarantee. They are "protected by the power of God" (1 Peter 1:5), such "that He who began a good work in [them] will perfect it until the day of Christ Jesus" (Phil. 1:6). That is why Paul could pray for the Thessalonians, "Now may the God of peace Himself sanctify you entirely; and may your spirit and soul and body be preserved complete, without blame at the coming of our Lord Jesus Christ. *Faithful is He who calls you, and He also will bring it to pass*" (1 Thess. 5:23–24; emphasis added). He would echo those same words in his second letter to that same church: "The Lord is faithful, and He will strengthen and protect you from the evil one" (2 Thess. 3:3). Jude similarly concluded his epistle with this triumphant doxology: "Now to Him who is *able to keep you from stumbling, and to make you stand in the presence of His glory blameless with great joy*, to the only God our Savior, through Jesus Christ our Lord, be glory, majesty, dominion and authority, before all time and now and forever. Amen" (vv. 24–25; emphasis added).

Promises like these underscore what we have already learned through our study of adoption. As those who have been made part of God's family, believers will be saved to the end. As the author of

---

24. E.g., John 3:36; 5:24; 6:47; 17:2, 12; 1 John 5:13.

Hebrews wrote of Christ, our Advocate, "Therefore He is able also to save forever those who draw near to God through Him, since He always lives to make intercession for them" (7:25; cf. 1 John 2:1).

Though the believer's salvation is guaranteed, the doctrine of *eternal security* is never an excuse to sin (Rom. 6:1). We are not liberated from sin in order to continue in it. Rather, we have been set free in order that we might "walk as children of Light" (Eph. 5:8), being "imitators of God, as beloved children" (v. 1). Moreover, we are sons of a new Father, subject to His authority and obligated, though out of love, to obey His commands. We are, to go back to our primary metaphor, *slaves* of righteousness.

By contrast, those who persist in unrepentant sin demonstrate that they have never truly been adopted into God's family, no matter what they profess (1 John 2:4–5). The true children of God inevitably manifest the character traits of their new family. Moreover, having been rescued from sin and adopted by God, their hearts are filled with gratitude and love for the Father who saved them. As eighteenth-century theologian John Gill explained:

> Nothing has a greater tendency to promote holiness of heart and life, than the absolute promises of God, respecting grace and glory, the assurance of adoption, the certainty of perseverance to the end, and the sure enjoyment of eternal life. . . . How preposterous and irrational must it be in a man who thinks himself to be a child of God, and believes he shall persevere to the end, from this consideration to indulge himself in all manner of sin.[25]

---

25. John Gill, *The Cause of God and Man* (London: Thomas Tegg & Son, 1888), 364–65.

Simultaneously Sons and Slaves

The marvelous doctrine of adoption assures us that, as believers in Jesus Christ, we are now and forever full-fledged members of God's family. Think of it! The only begotten Son of God took on the form of a slave (Phil. 2:7), so that the slaves of sin might become both slaves of righteousness and sons of God! As Alexander Maclaren explains,

> The Servant-Son makes us slaves and sons. . . . [A]nd if you will trust yourselves to Him, and give your hearts to Him, and ask Him to govern you, He will govern you; and if you will abandon your false liberty which is servitude, and take the sober freedom which is obedience, then He will bring you to share in His [blessings] of joyful service; and even we may be able to say, "My meat and my drink is to do the will of Him that sent me," and truly saying that, we shall have the key to all delights.[26]

In Christ, we are no longer children of wrath and disobedience but are instead children of righteousness, submitting ourselves to our heavenly Father, whose holy character we are called and empowered to imitate.[27] Through Christ we have been set free. We are no longer slaves to sin, to the fear of death, or to the condemnation of the law.[28] But we have been made slaves *of* God, *for* Christ, *to* righteousness.[29]

---

26. Alexander Maclaren, *Expositions of Holy Scripture, the Acts* (n.p., BiblioLife, 2007), 149, commenting on Acts 4:26, 27, 29.

27. Cf. Matt. 12:50; John 12:36; Eph. 5:1, 8; 2 Tim. 1:9; 1 Peter 1:14–16.

28. Cf. John 8:34–36; Rom. 8:15–17; Gal. 4:3–7; Heb. 2:15.

29. Rom. 6:18; 1 Cor. 7:23; Gal. 5:24; cf. James 1:1; Rom. 1:1.

Such is true freedom. Thus, we are simultaneously *sons* and *slaves*. The two realities are not mutually exclusive—even if the metaphors are different.[30] Forever we will be part of His family. Forever we will be in His glorious servitude (Rev. 22:3).

---

30. In John 15:15, during His Upper Room discourse, Jesus told His disciples, "No longer do I call you slaves . . . but I have called you friends." At first glance, it seems as if He might be obliterating the slave metaphor altogether. But such is not the case, as evidenced by the fact that the disciples continued to refer to themselves as "slaves of Christ" long afterwards (e.g., Peter in 2 Peter 1:1 and John in Revelation 1:1). Moreover, Jesus defined friendship as submission to Him: "You are My friends if you do what I command you" (John 15:14). In John 15:15, Jesus' point was simply that, by revealing to the disciples all that He was doing, He was treating them not merely as slaves but also as friends and confidants (since slaves are not privy to knowing what the Master is doing). That Jesus views believers as both friends and slaves is supported by a host of New Testament passages. (See also Harris, *Slave of Christ* [Downers Grove, IL: InterVarsity Press, 1999], 144–6).

twelve

Ready to Meet the Master

W hen Lamon, a slave farmer on the Greek isle of Lesvos, heard that his master would be coming for a visit, he immediately sprang into action.

"Lamon got his master's country house ready to please the eye in every way. He cleaned out the springs so that they could have clean water, carted the dung out of the farmyard so that it wouldn't annoy them with its smell, and worked on the enclosed garden so that it could be seen in all its beauty."[1] Lamon further instructed his son "to fatten up the goats as much as possible, saying that the master would certainly look at them." Nothing could be left to chance. Though Lamon and his family had always tended the master's country estate, the stakes were higher now than ever. The master was coming to personally inspect the farm.

Imagine Lamon's horror when he discovered that the garden of fruit trees, flowers, and vines had been vandalized. What would the master say when he saw the devastation? Surely, Lamon would be severely scourged, perhaps even hanged. The master did not visit often. But when he did, there were no excuses for mismanagement.

The story of Lamon and his family, written by a second-century Greek playwright, is fictional. Nonetheless, it accurately captures the

1. Quoted in Keith Bradley, *Slavery and Society at Rome* (Cambridge University Press, 1994), 103.

anticipation and "anxiety that a visit of inspection from the slaveowner might induce among his slaves."[2] For rustic slaves, who did not see their owners very often, the master's arrival was especially important. For many months, or even years, they had been commanded to work in his absence. Now, in the moment of his arrival, they would either be rewarded or reprimanded for their efforts. All depended on the master's approval and on whether or not the slaves had been diligent and wise while he was away.

The Master's Return

In Matthew 25, Jesus painted a similar word picture for His disciples. He began the parable like this: "[The kingdom of heaven] is just like a man about to go on a journey, who called his own slaves and entrusted his possessions to them. To one he gave five talents, to another, two, and to another, one, each according to his own ability; and he went on his journey. . . . Now after a long time the master of those slaves came and settled accounts with them" (vv. 14–15, 19).

The slaves in Jesus' story are urban slaves—domestic stewards who had been given the responsibility of managing the master's estate in his absence. Yet the situation is similar to that of a rustic slave anticipating his master's arrival. In both cases, the master is away for a prolonged period. While he is gone, he expects the slaves to supervise his estate and further his interests. When he returns, he will inspect their work and either praise or punish them as a result.

---

2. Ibid., 103. The author parallels this fictional play with the writings of Pliny the Younger, demonstrating the accuracy of "its slave psychology [which] is drawn from contemporary reality" (105).

In our Lord's parable, two of the slaves applied themselves diligently to their task. Each of them doubled the amount of money they had received. When the master finally returned, he was exceedingly pleased with the work they had done. Thus, his commendation: "Well done, good and faithful slave. You were faithful with a few things, I will put you in charge of many things; enter into the joy of your master" (vv. 21, 23).

But the third slave squandered his opportunity to invest—having hidden his portion in a hole in the ground. The master's displeasure resounded in words of condemnation: "You wicked, lazy slave, . . . you ought to have put my money in the bank, and on my arrival I would have received my money back with interest. Therefore take away the talent from him, and give it to the one who has the ten talents" (vv. 26–28). While these words were still ringing in his ears, the worthless slave was thrown "into the outer darkness; in that place there will be weeping and gnashing of teeth" (v. 30).

The imagery is clear. The master represents Christ, and his prolonged absence pictures the time between Christ's ascension and His second coming. The slaves are professing believers who have been entrusted, as stewards, with various resources, abilities, blessings, and opportunities. One day, they will all be called to give an account for that stewardship.[3]

That the first two slaves represent true believers becomes quickly

---

3. As W. D. Davies and Dale C. Allison Jr. have explained, "This parable, like the preceding, is filled with obvious symbols. The master is Jesus. His slaves represent the [visible] church, whose members have received various responsibilities. The master's departure is the departure of the earthly Jesus. The long time of the master's absence is the age of the church. His return is the *parousia* of the Son of man. The rewards given to the good slaves stand for heavenly rewards given to the faithful at the great assize, and their joy is that of the messianic banquet" (*The Gospel According to Saint Matthew*, vol. 3, ICC [Edinburgh: T&T Clark, 2000], 402).

apparent in the parable. Though they received different amounts of money to manage—each in accordance with his ability—they both invested wisely, worked diligently, and demonstrated their faithfulness to the master. Similarly, believers have each been entrusted with different abilities and opportunities. We are called to be faithful with what we have been given, knowing that "each will receive his own reward according to his own labor" (1 Cor. 3:8). To hear our Master say, "Well done!" and welcome us into heaven is the greatest reward we could ever receive. As faithful slaves in this life, we will be given even greater opportunities to serve in heaven. Such is implied by Jesus' parallel parable in Luke 19:11–27, where the king grants governing authority over parts of his kingdom as a reward to his dutiful slaves (vv. 17, 19). Likewise, we look forward to reigning with Christ as part of our heavenly reward.[4]

The third slave represents a person who claims to be a Christian but in reality serves only himself. Lazy and foolish, he squandered the opportunities he was given. His response to the master showed that he had no love for him or his estate. He even accused the master of being harsh and exacting (v. 21), yet his actions betrayed the truth of that allegation.[5] If he had really feared his master so much, he would have worked hard while the master was gone. Instead, he lazily and selfishly served himself, while irresponsibly putting his master's money in the ground and forgetting about it. Though he did not actually embezzle

---

4. Cf. Rom. 5:17; 2 Tim. 2:12; Rev. 2:26–27; 3:21.

5. Speaking of all of Jesus' parables involving slaves, Michael Card has observed: "The slave parables of Jesus teach us that, beyond all doubt, the Master is not a 'hard man,' but rather one of immeasurable mercy, someone who cancels million-dollar debts with the wave of his hand. He is the Master who dresses himself to serve and wash the feet of his slaves. He is the One who is willing to suffer and die with and for his servants. But finally, and it must be said, he is a Lord who expects simple, trusting obedience, not based on wage or reward but simply on the knowledge of who our Master is" (*A Better Freedom* [Downers Grove, IL: InterVarsity Press, 2009], 116).

any money, his wicked actions cost the master a great deal—since his investment failed to produce any profit whatsoever. This evidenced the fact that he was not merely unfaithful; he was also faithless—an unbeliever who is ultimately cast into hell.

The implications are hard to miss—especially in light of the first-century slave/master imagery on which the story is built. The Master is currently away, but He will be returning soon.[6] Opportunity abounds, but time is running out. When He arrives, He will judge His slaves. Those who have demonstrated faithfulness to Him (thereby evidencing the genuineness of their conversion) will be rewarded with His pleasure and welcomed into heaven. Those who have squandered every resource (thereby evidencing the true condition of their hard hearts) will receive divine condemnation and punishment.

Though we do not know when the Master will return, we do know one thing for certain: *one day He will come back* (Mark 13:33–37). That simple fact should motivate us to greater holiness and service.[7] It should also comfort and enthuse us, if we are living obediently. A slave only fears the master's return if he has been unfaithful. But for Christ's slaves who have worked hard and served well, the Master's arrival is a moment of great celebration. For them, His coming represents entrance into His joy and the beginning of great reward.

The Judgment Seat of Christ

The parable of the talents in Matthew 25 specifically refers to our Lord's judgment at His second coming (cf. Rev. 11:18). But the Scripture

---

6. Hence our Lord's promise in Rev. 3:11 and 22:12, 20.

7. 1 John 2:28, 3:2–3; cf. Titus 2:11–13.

teaches that all believers from every generation of human history will appear before Christ. Knowing this, the apostle Paul made it his goal, in all of life, "to be pleasing to Him. For we must all appear before the judgment seat of Christ, so that each one may be recompensed for his deeds in the body, according to what he has done, whether good or bad" (2 Cor. 5:9–10). Elsewhere, he told the Christians in Rome, "We shall all stand before the judgment seat of Christ. For it is written, '*As I live, says the Lord, every knee shall bow to me, and every tongue shall confess to God.*' So then each of us shall give account of himself to God" (Rom. 14:10–12 NKJV).

Whether by death or by rapture, every believer will one day report to the heavenly Master for evaluation and reward. Once again, the obedient slave has nothing to fear from facing the Master. As R. C. H. Lenski observed, "He who, as a slave to Christ, submits his will to him in all he does 'is well-pleasing to God' and need never fear to stand before his judgment seat."[8]

On the other hand, those believers who spend their lives in temporal and worthless pursuits should expect minimal reward from Christ. The sins of every believer are, of course, forever forgiven through the Cross; salvation cannot be forfeited. Yet those who squander their God-given opportunities for spiritual service will one day discover that their works consist of little more than wood, hay, and stubble. Lacking any eternal value, such works will not stand up under the fire of God's scrutiny (see 1 Corinthians 3:12–15). The fear of His displeasure, counterbalanced by the promise of His reward, is a powerful motivation for enduring faithfulness. In the same way that first-century slaves

---

8. R. C. H. Lenski, *Interpretation of Saint Paul's Epistle to the Romans 8–16* (Minneapolis, Augsburg Fortress, 2008), 843.

were accountable to their human masters, Christ's slaves are ultimately accountable to Him.

The apostle Paul used that same imagery when speaking directly to physical slaves and their human owners. In Ephesians 6:5–9, he wrote:

> Slaves, be obedient to those who are your masters according to the flesh, with fear and trembling, in the sincerity of your heart, as to Christ; not by way of eyeservice, as men-pleasers, but as slaves of Christ, doing the will of God from the heart. With good will render service, as to the Lord, and not to men, knowing that whatever good thing each one does, this he will receive back from the Lord, whether slave or free. And masters, do the same things to them, and give up threatening, knowing that both their Master and yours is in heaven, and there is no partiality with Him.

Every believer, whether slave or free, has a Master in heaven. He is a perfect and impartial Judge, and one day we will each stand before Him to give an account.

The certainty of that future reality emboldened Paul to preach the gospel no matter the consequences. After all, he had been appointed to do so by the commandment of God Himself (Titus 1:3). Though he would often be rejected and persecuted, Paul was far more concerned with obeying his divine calling than with gaining man's approval. Only one thing mattered—pleasing the Master.

When he was falsely accused, his response was simple: "To me it is a very small thing that I may be examined by you, or by any human court; in fact, I do not even examine myself. For I am conscious of nothing against myself, yet I am not by this acquitted; but the one who examines me is the Lord" (1 Cor. 4:3–4). When imprisoned and awaiting death, "his thoughts [were] now consumed by the glorious destiny that awaits the 'slave of Christ.'"[9] At the close of his life, as he sat alone in a Roman dungeon, Paul could still smile at the future. Words of hope pervaded his perspective because he measured success by a heavenly standard. Thus, he wrote to Timothy, "I have fought the good fight, I have finished the course, I have kept the faith; in the future there is laid up for me the crown of righteousness, which the Lord, the righteous Judge, will award to me on that day; and not only to me, but also to all who have loved His appearing" (2 Tim. 4:7–8).

Contrast that with those who waste their lives in empty pursuits. In his book *Don't Waste Your Life*, John Piper tells of a couple who took an early retirement in order to settle in Florida and live out their days cruising on their yacht, playing softball, and collecting seashells. In response to that kind of life, Piper commented:

> I thought it might be a joke. A spoof on the American Dream. But it wasn't. Tragically, this was the dream: Come to the end of your life—your one and only precious, God-given life—and let the last great work of your life, before you give an account to your Creator, be this: playing softball and collecting shells. Picture them before Christ at the great day of judgment: "Look, Lord. See my shells." *That* is a tragedy. And people today are spending billions of dollars to persuade you to embrace that tragic dream. Over against that, I put my protest: Don't buy it. Don't waste your life.[10]

---

9. Mark Edwards, "Paul, St.," 542–43 in *Encyclopedia of Ancient Greece*, ed. Nigel Guy Wilson (New York: Routledge, 2006).

10. John Piper, *Don't Waste Your Life* (Wheaton, IL: Crossway, 2007), 45–46.

Such is a timely warning—especially in our consumer-driven culture—for all who desire to live "sensibly, righteously and godly in the present age" (Titus 2:12). As slaves to Christ, we must "walk in a manner worthy of the calling with which [we] have been called" (Eph. 4:1). Our obedience and sacrificial service in this life will not go unnoticed or unrewarded by our sovereign Lord.[11] Even if our faithfulness to Him is costly and painful, we can rejoice in knowing that this "momentary, light affliction is producing for us an eternal weight of glory far beyond all comparison" (2 Cor. 4:17). Our faith will soon be turned to sight, and we will see our Master face-to-face. On that day, what an indescribable joy it will be to hear His gracious words of welcome: "Well done, My good and faithful slave. Enter into the joy of your Master."

Living on Earth as Citizens of Heaven

As we have seen, the New Testament uses a number of metaphors to highlight the believer's changed status in Christ—including the images of a slave and a son. We were formerly slaves to sin, but now we are slaves of Christ. We were once sons of disobedience and wrath, but we have been adopted into God's family as children of righteousness. But there is a third word picture that we also need to consider—especially as we reflect on the fact that our true home is in heaven. It is the image of a *citizen*.

Even though we have not yet been there, we are citizens of heaven. We once walked according to the prince of this world, but at conversion

---

11. Matt. 5:12; 10:42.

we were transferred into the kingdom of Christ. As a result, we no longer align ourselves with this wicked world system, to which we have become foreigners and sojourners. Instead, our self-identity is found in our allegiance to the King of kings and in our affinity with His people.

From Slaves to Citizens

It was not uncommon in the first century for a Roman slave to eventually be granted his freedom and, as a result, to receive citizenship.[12] Under Roman law, "formal manumission by a Roman citizen master normally gave citizenship to the ex-slave."[13] Thus, the slaves of Roman citizens, once liberated, became Roman citizens themselves.

Slaves could be officially set free, or formally manumitted, in two primary ways. The owner could wait until his death to free his slaves, in which case he would make provision for their release in his last will and testament. This was known as "manumission by testament" (*testamenta*). Or, if a master wished to liberate his slaves while he was still living, he would employ "manumission by rod" (*vindicta*).[14] Manumission by rod

---

12. Author Jane F. Gardner notes that this practice was unique to ancient Rome: "The fact has aroused comment, both in ancient times and in modern times, that, unlike the rest of the Greco-Roman world, the Romans normally gave slaves citizenship upon manumission" (*Being a Roman Citizen* [New York: Routledge, 1993], 7).

13. James Albert Harrill, *The Manumission of Slaves in Early Christianity* (Tubingen: J. C. B. Mohr Siebeck, 1995), 171. William D. Phillips, in *Slavery from Roman Times to the Early Transatlantic Trade* (University of Minnesota Press, 1985), 30, notes exceptions to this. Jennifer A. Glancy observes similar exceptions, but in the end concludes: "Nonetheless, many slaves were fortunate enough to spend at least a few final years of their lives not only as freedpersons but also citizens" (*Slavery in Early Christianity* [Minneapolis: Fortress Press, 2006], 95).

14. A third type of manumission ("manumission by census") was only possible when a Roman census was being taken, and involved an assertion on the part of the owner that his slave should be counted, not as a slave, but as one who had been freed. However, this method was no longer in use during New Testament times. (See Scott Bartchy, *First-Century Slavery* [Eugene, OR: Wipf and Stock Publishers, 2002], 92.)

involved a symbolic ceremony performed before the local civil magistrate, in which "a third party asserted that the slave was a free man, and touched him with a rod (*vindicta*), so rejecting the owner's claim to ownership; the owner offered no defense; the magistrate then awarded the suit in favor of the plaintiff, and declared the slave a free man."[15]

Though the ex-slave was now liberated, he was never entirely independent from the one who set him free. As Murray J. Harris explains, "He was permanently obliged to render certain services (*operae*) to his former master, now his patron (*patronus*), tasks related to his former employment and performed on a specified number of days each month or year."[16] On the flip side, the patron also had certain legal obligations to the former slave. If the ex-slave was in desperate need, the patron was bound to provide him with food and shelter. Moreover, the patron could not testify against his freedman in a criminal court.[17] Added to this, a critical change in relationship took place at the point of manumission: "A slave had no father in the eyes of Roman law, so when he was freed his former master was recognized as his legal father."[18]

Once emancipated and granted citizenship, the former slave enjoyed many new privileges—including the rights to buy and sell property, marry a Roman citizen, and make a Roman will.[19] "In general

---

15. Gardner, *Being a Roman Citizen*, 9.

16. Murray J. Harris, *Slave of Christ* [Downers Grove, IL: InterVarsity Press, 1999], 72. On this point, Francis Lyall adds, "A fundamental difference existed between the freed and the freeborn. The former was still to a degree subject to his former owner—his patron" (*Slaves, Citizens, Sons: Legal Metaphors in the Epistles* [Grand Rapids: Academie Books, 1984], 43).

17. Cf. Lyall, *Slaves, Citizens, Sons*, 44.

18. James Jeffers, *The Greco-Roman World of the New Testament* (Downers Grove, IL: InterVarsity Press, 1999), 239.

19. Various informal methods of emancipation also took place, though they did not result in the legal citizenship of the former slave (cf. Harris, *Slave of Christ*, 72).

Roman citizenship meant the right to vote; the right to hold property and make contracts; freedom from torture; special protections from the death penalty; and equal treatment under Roman law."[20] The change in position was both immediate and striking: "This sudden and dramatic change of status was a remarkable phenomenon. Overnight, and by the wave of the hand, so to speak, a rank outsider became a genuine insider."[21]

Citizenship brought with it not only numerous advantages but also a sense of civic responsibility—including the possibility of military or civil service.[22] In exchange for their privileged status, citizens were expected to show loyalty and obedience to the state: "What, then, did it entail being a citizen of Rome? At its heart the status meant that the individual lived under [both] the guidance and protection of Roman law."[23] Moreover, in an ancient Roman context, citizenship was far more than a superficial association with one's country of origin. It was, in fact, an integral part of one's very self-identity:

> The conception of citizenship among the ancient Greeks and Romans was deeper than among ourselves. We can think of human existence and life apart from citizenship, but to the ancient member of a πόλις [polis] or a civitas ["town" or "city"] citizenship was life and life was

---

20. Amy Chua, Day of Empire (New York: Doubleday, 2007), 45.

21. Harris, Slave of Christ, 72. Along these same lines, Keith Bradley notes that "formal manumission meant that the slave was set free and simultaneously given Roman citizenship—was admitted at once, that is to say, into the Roman civic community, a very radical transformation of status" (Slavery and Society at Rome, 155).

22. Everett Ferguson, in Backgrounds of Early Christianity (Grand Rapids: Eerdmans, 2003), explains that "under the Republic [509 B.C. to 28 B.C.] citizenship had carried certain duties, especially the possibility of military service, but under the principate [27 B.C. to A.D. 284] such duties were increasingly severed from citizenship" (63).

23. Derek Benjamin Heater, A Brief History of Citizenship (New York: New York University Press, 2004), 31.

citizenship. This explains why St. Paul could use πολιτεύεσθαι [*politeuesthai*, "to behave as a citizen"] practically in the sense of "to live" (Acts 23:1; Php 1:27; cf. 3:20 πολίτευμα [*politeuma*, 'citizenship']). The life of a city is a development out of the more primitive life of the village-community (κώμη, *uicus*). A πόλις in fact consists of a number of κωμαι [*komai*, 'communities'], each of which consists of a number of families (οἶκος, *domus*). The unity was generally based on blood-relationship.[24]

In other words, the family relationships from which ancient communities and villages—and eventually towns, cities, and nations—emerged, cemented the loyalty of the citizens to their homeland and to their fellow countrymen. To be a citizen was, in a very real sense, to be part of an extended family.

The Parallel to Heavenly Citizenship

The imagery of citizenship conveys a number of important truths about the Christian life—especially in light of first-century slavery and manumission. Declared by God to be free at the moment of our salvation, we were instantaneously liberated from sin and ushered into the wonder and privilege of full citizenship in the kingdom of His beloved Son (Col. 1:13). Though we no longer have any obligation to our former master (sin/Satan), we do have an obligation to serve the One who set us free—namely, Christ Himself. He is our *Patron*, and we are His freedmen.[25] And just as the patron could bring no legal charge against his freedman, so also Christ will never condemn those

---

24. A. Souter, in *Dictionary of the Apostolic Church*, vol. 1, ed. James Hastings (New York: Charles Scribner's Sons, 1919), s.v. "Citizenship," 212.

25. 1 Cor. 7:22; cf. John 8:32, 36; Rom. 8:2, 12–14.

who belong to Him.[26]

Though we were previously enemies and strangers to God, we are now citizens of heaven[27] and "fellow citizens with the saints" (Eph. 2:19). We are no longer subject to our sinful passions; now we are subjects of our heavenly King. He is simultaneously our Master, our Patron, our Father, and our sovereign Prince.

Of course, our heavenly citizenship is founded not only in our manumission from sin but also in the reality of our new birth. As Jesus explained to Nicodemus in John 3:3, entrance into the kingdom of God is granted only to those who are first "born again," or literally, "born from above." It is through this new birth that sinners are made God's children, for He has "brought us forth by the word of truth" (James 1:18).[28] Those who have been born of God are characterized by overcoming the world through faith, showing love to others, and demonstrating obedience to the Lord.[29]

Therefore we are citizens of heaven, both by emancipation and by birth, and all by grace. As such, we enjoy infinite privilege as well as great responsibility. We possess all of the innumerable advantages of knowing God, walking in His ways, worshipping Him, and relating to Him as both our King and our Father. Heaven's law is our law; heaven's interests are our interests; and heaven's citizens are our fellow citizens. As ambassadors of His kingdom,[30] we can approach this life with a supernatural confidence that stems from an eternal mind-set. As one author has explained:

---

26. Cf. Rom. 8:1, 33–34; Heb. 7:25; 1 John 2:1.

27. Phil. 3:20; cf. 1 Peter 2:11.

28. Cf. John 1:12–13; 1 Peter 1:3–4, 23.

29. 1 John 2:29; 4:7; 5:4.

30. Cf. 2 Cor. 5:18–21; Eph. 6:19–20.

The Christian is subject to the jurisdiction of heaven and possesses the privileges of that citizenship. His home state will protect him and his interests, will intervene on his behalf, and will itself determine his rights and duties. The Christian is therefore in one sense to a degree, in another sense completely, free from duties imposed by the local law of the world, his temporary residence, which, after all, exists only by the permission of the dominant power, Heaven.[31]

By the same token, there is an incredible responsibility that comes with being part of Christ's kingdom. As His subjects, we must properly represent Him. Accordingly, we are commanded to "walk in a manner worthy of the God who calls you into His own kingdom and glory" (1 Thess. 2:12). The author of Hebrews similarly wrote, "Since we receive a kingdom which cannot be shaken, let us show gratitude, by which we may offer to God an acceptable service with reverence and awe" (12:28).

As citizens of heaven, we are now part of Christ's church, His *ekklesia*. The term itself means "those who are called out" and originally referred to the citizens of a city who were "called out to do battle for the protection of the community, and from that meaning it came also to be used to mean the assembly of the citizens met to transact the affairs of the community."[32] When we apply this understanding to the Christian *ekklesia*, we learn that "the church is the assembly of the citizens of heaven, met according to the summons of the chief citizen, and met to do business either by way of government of the affairs of the

---

31. Lyall, *Slaves, Citizens, Sons*, 63.

32. Ibid., 66.

community, or to defend its interests."[33] Put simply, the corporate gathering of believers is an assembly of heaven's citizens and Christ's slaves, united in purpose and in loving loyalty to their Master and King.

Our life is synonymous with our citizenship. Our priorities, passions, and pursuits have all been changed because our very identity has been transformed (Phil. 1:21). Like the saints of old, we no longer chase after the passing pleasures of this world.[34] Instead, our eyes are fixed on heaven, our true home, the place where Christ is.[35] Whether we go to Him in death or He comes to us in rapture, we will soon be together with Him forever.[36]

One day we will stand in His presence, as slaves before the Master. One day we will bow before Him, as subjects before the King. As both slaves and citizens, we will serve Him and reign with Him for all eternity. The apostle John, in his final description of the eternal state, emphasized this twofold reality. Noting the glories that await every believer, he wrote:

> The throne of God and of the Lamb will be in [the New Jerusalem], and His bond-servants [*douloi*, literally, *slaves*] will serve Him; they will see His face, and His name will be on their foreheads. And there will no longer be any night; and they will not have need of the light of a lamp nor the light of the sun, because the Lord God will illumine them; and they will reign [with Him] forever and ever. (Rev. 22:3–5)

---

33. Ibid.

34. Cf. Heb. 11:16, 26; 1 John 2:16–17.

35. Cf. Heb. 12:22–24; Col. 3:1.

36. Cf. 2 Cor. 5:8; 1 Thess. 4:17.

thirteen

The Riches of the Paradox

While nothing in the Bible is contradictory, many of the Bible's most provocative and profound truths appear to us paradoxical. Consider, for example, the truth that salvation is both free and costly, or that to be truly rich you must be poor in spirit, or that to find your life you must lose it, or that to be wise you must embrace the foolishness of the gospel.[1] Scripture teaches that those who mourn will be comforted; those who give will receive; those who are least will be greatest; those who are humble will be exalted; and those who are last will be first.[2] We learn, further, that God uses evil for good; that He is three yet one; and that Jesus Christ, the second member of the Trinity, is simultaneously fully God and fully man.[3] These are just some of the wondrous mysteries that the Bible sets forth.

To this list, we could certainly add the biblical teaching regarding slavery to Christ. A metaphor commonly associated with scorn, oppression, and abuse, *slavery* has been gloriously transformed, in Christ, to signify honor, liberty, and eternal bliss! As one writer explains,

> Like the cross, slavery is both paradigm and paradox. The cross, the most excruciating and pervasive symbol of suffering and death in the

---

1. Cf. Matt. 5:3; 13:44–46; Luke 17:33; 1 Cor. 3:18.

2. Cf. Matt. 5:4; 23:12; 20:16; Luke 22:26; Acts 20:35.

3. Cf. Gen. 50:20; Deut. 6:4; Matt. 28:19; John 1:1, 14; Heb. 1:3; 4:15.

first century, has come to represent for the followers of Jesus the only way to peace and life. In the same sense slavery, which represents the total denial of freedom, becomes for the follower of Christ, the Servant Savior, the only means to the realization of the true freedom. . . . [Jesus] came in the form of a slave, not to offer us freedom from slavery but a new kind of slavery that is freedom.[4]

Over the last twelve chapters, we've considered both the biblical and historical basis for this profound paradigm. We have considered the crucial difference between *servants* and *slaves*—noting that while servants are hired, slaves are owned. Believers are not merely Christ's hired servants; they are His slaves, belonging to Him as His possession. He is their Owner and Master, worthy of their unquestioned allegiance and absolute obedience. His Word is their final authority; His will, their ultimate mandate. Having taken up their cross to follow Him, they have died to themselves and can now say with Paul, "I have been crucified with Christ; and it is no longer I who live, but Christ lives in me" (Gal. 2:20). As the apostle elsewhere explained, "[Christ] died for all, so that they who live might no longer live for themselves, but for Him who died and rose again on their behalf" (2 Cor. 5:15).

We have also examined the biblical teaching about Christ's lordship. He is both our Lord and our God. He is the King over every individual believer, over His entire church, and over every created thing. Though unbelievers reject His authority in this life, there will come a day when "EVERY KNEE WILL BOW" and "every tongue will confess that Jesus Christ is Lord" (Phil. 2:10–11). We, too, will one day

---

4. Michael Card, *A Better Freedom* (Downers Grove, IL: InterVarsity Press, 2009), 23–24.

give an account to Him, and He will reward us for our faithfulness. How we long to hear those words of blessing and commendation, "Well done, My good and faithful slave. Enter into the joy of your Master."

Our study of slavery has reminded us that we were once the wretched slaves of the cruelest master imaginable—sin. As members of a fallen human race, we were bound, blind, and dead in our disobedience and rebellion. It was in the midst of our helplessness and hopelessness that God intervened. Being rich in mercy, He chose us, set His love on us, and rescued us from the clutches of our former owner. Through Christ's sacrificial death, we were redeemed from the slave market of sin. God cleansed us from our iniquity, clothed us in His righteousness, and welcomed us into His household forever.

But our gracious God did not stop there. He made us not only slaves to righteousness but also citizens in His kingdom, friends around His table, and even adopted children in His family. Now, we who once were not a people have become the people of God; we who were formerly "far off have been brought near by the blood of Christ" (Eph. 2:13); we who had no hope can look forward to the heavenly inheritance He has promised to all who are His own. Such a glorious transformation is possible only because Christ Himself took on "the form of a slave" (Phil. 2:7 HCSB) so that He might die to redeem the slaves of sin and reconcile them to God. In response, we will praise His glorious name forever and ever, as we join with the choirs of heaven, singing, "Worthy are You to take the book and to break its seals; for You were slain, and purchased for God with Your blood men from every tribe and tongue and people and nation. . . . Worthy is the Lamb that was slain to receive power and riches and wisdom and might and honor and glory and blessing" (Rev. 5:9, 12).

Four Compelling Paradoxes

Clearly, we could never fully exhaust the glorious realities of slavery to Christ. In fact, we never will—for as we have seen, we will worship and serve Him as His slaves for all eternity (Rev. 19:5; 22:3). Like the facet of an exquisite diamond, every angle of this profound biblical metaphor adds new dimension, beauty, and insight. Sadly, its riches have largely been lost in translation, at least in the English-speaking world. But for those who are willing to dig beneath the surface, a theological treasure awaits—one that showcases the glories of our salvation in a remarkable way. The doctrines of grace all take on fuller meaning when seen through the lens of slavery, a lens familiar to and intended by the New Testament writers.

In reality, all of life should be viewed from that perspective. As Christians, *we are slaves of Christ*. What a radical difference that truth should make in our daily lives! We no longer live for ourselves. Rather, we make it our aim to please the Master in everything. With that in mind, let's consider the following four paradoxes of slavery to Christ— each of which provides another dimension of the glorious calling with which we have been called (Eph. 4:1).

Slavery Brings Freedom

As shocking as it is profound, God's Word teaches that true freedom can only be found through slavery to Christ. Though they think they are free, all unbelievers are in reality slaves to sin—held captive to their lusts and ensnared in their trespasses. In fact, the Bible denotes only two categories of people in this world: those who are slaves to sin and those who are slaves to righteousness. Paul contrasted those two groups in Romans 6:

Do you not know that when you present yourselves to someone as slaves for obedience, you are slaves of the one whom you obey, either of sin resulting in death, or of obedience resulting in righteousness? But thanks be to God that though you were slaves of sin, you became obedient from the heart to that form of teaching to which you were committed, and having been freed from sin, you became slaves of righteousness. (vv. 16–18)

As the apostle shows in this passage, there is no such thing as absolute moral independence. Every person is a slave—either to sin or to God. James Montgomery Boice articulated this reality with these words:

> *There is no such thing as absolute freedom for anyone.* No human is free to do everything he or she may want to do. There is one being in the universe who is *totally* free, of course. That is God. But all others are limited by or enslaved by someone or something. As a result, the only meaningful question in this area is: Who or what are you serving? . . . Since you and I are human beings and not God, we can never be autonomous. We must either be slaves to sin or slaves of Jesus Christ. But here is the wonderful and very striking thing: *To be a slave of Jesus Christ is true freedom.*[5]

Slavery to Christ not only means freedom *from* sin, guilt, and condemnation. It also means freedom *to* obey, *to* please God, and *to* live the way our Creator intended us to live—in intimate fellowship with

---

5. James Montgomery Boice, *Romans*, 4 vols. (Grand Rapids: Baker, 1991), 2:689–90; emphasis in original. Cf. Douglas Moo, *The Wycliffe Exegetical Commentary, Romans 1–8* (Chicago: Moody Press, 1991), 415, where he wrote, "One is never free from a master, and those non-Christians who think they are free are under an illusion created and sustained by Satan."

Him. Thus, "having been freed from sin [we have been] enslaved to God" (Rom. 6:22; cf. 1 Peter 2:16). Slavery to Christ, then, is the only freedom, for "if the Son makes you free, you will be free indeed" (John 8:36). As Alexander Maclaren has explained:

> Such slavery is the only freedom. Liberty does not mean doing as you like, it means liking as you ought, and doing that. He only is free who submits to God in Christ, and thereby overcomes himself and the world and all antagonism, and is able to do that which it is his life to do. . . . You talk about the bondage of obedience. Ah! "the weight of too much liberty" is a far sorer bondage. They are the slaves who say, "Let us break His bonds asunder, and cast away His cords from us"; and they are the free men who say, "Lord, put Thy blessed shackles on my arms, and impose Thy will upon my will, and fill my heart with Thy love; and then will and hands will move freely and delightedly." "If the Son makes you free, ye shall be free indeed."[6]

Though Christians do fall into sin from time to time, through their own disobedient choices, they are never again the slaves of sin as they were before being rescued by Christ and set free. Sin no longer has the power to control them. Fourth-century church father John Chrysostom vividly illustrated this point when he wrote:

> It is absurd for those who are being led toward the kingdom of God to have sin ruling over them or for those who are called to reign with Christ to choose to be captives to sin, as if one should throw down the crown from off his head and choose to be the slave of a hysterical

---

6. Alexander Maclaren, *Expositions of Holy Scripture, the Acts* (n.p.: Bibliolife, 2007), 148.

woman who comes begging and covered in rags. . . . How is it that sin can reign in you? It is not from any power of its own but only from your laziness.[7]

Having been redeemed by Christ and empowered by the Holy Spirit, believers have everything they need to gain victory over temptation and sin. The power of sin has been permanently broken. The condemnation of the Law has been forever removed. The freedom of obedience is ours to possess. Now "we serve in newness of the Spirit" (Rom. 7:6). In being Christ's slaves, we are finally and fully liberated; in submitting to Him we experience true emancipation, for His law has forever set us free from the law of sin and death (Rom. 8:2).

Slavery Ends Prejudice

Not only is slavery to Christ the way to true freedom; it is also the path to reconciliation and unity within the body of Christ. When believers realize that they are all *slaves*, called to model the humility of the ultimate slave (Phil. 2:5–7), it becomes obvious how they ought to treat others: "Do nothing from selfishness or empty conceit, but with humility of mind regard one another as more important than yourselves" (v. 3). As our Lord told His disciples, "Whoever wishes to be first among you shall be slave of all. For even the Son of Man did not come to be served, but to serve, and to give His life a ransom for many" (Mark 10:44–45). After performing a slave's job by washing the disciples' feet, Jesus reminded them, "If I then, the Lord and the Teacher, washed your feet, you also ought to wash one another's feet. For I gave you an example that you also should do as I did to you. Truly, truly, I

---

7. Chrysostom, *Homilies on Romans*, 11, quoted in Gerald Bray, ed. *Romans, Ancient Christian Commentary on Scripture* (Downers Grove, IL: InterVarsity, 1998), 163.

say to you, a slave is not greater than his master, nor is one who is sent greater than the one who sent him. If you know these things, you are blessed if you do them" (John 13:14–17). Sacrificial service and love for one another ought to characterize the followers of Christ. After all, every one of us is a slave, called to imitate the selfless example of our Master Himself.

As the gospel went forth from Israel to Samaria and then to the Gentiles, it broke down previous prejudices between different social classes and racial groups. Jews and Gentiles, men and women, slaves and freemen—all were welcomed into the church, where they enjoyed equal spiritual standing before God as citizens of heaven and fellow slaves of Christ. The gospel had put an end to all prior prejudices. As Paul told the Colossians, "Put on the new self who is being renewed to a true knowledge according to the image of the One who created him—a renewal in which there is no distinction between Greek and Jew, circumcised and uncircumcised, barbarian, Scythian, slave and freeman, but Christ is all, and in all" (3:10–11).

But those transformed by the gospel were more than just fellow slaves. Having been adopted by God as His children, they were now members of the same family. Their new relationship to one another was stronger than any previous bonds or relations. The New Testament church was "more a family than an ecclesiastical association or organization. Such fellow feeling does away with considerations of race (Gal. 3:28; cf. Col. 3:11). Paul, the Jew, speaks of Titus, the Greek (Gal. 2:3), as his brother (2 Cor. 2:13) and uses the same term of Philemon, another Greek, and of Onesimus, a runaway slave (Philem. 16, 20)."[8]

Of these examples, Paul's treatment of Onesimus is perhaps the

---

8. Francis Lyall, *Slaves, Citizens, Sons: Legal Metaphors in the Epistles* (Grand Rapids: Academie Books, 1984), 129–30.

most remarkable. The apostle fully embraced this Gentile runaway slave without prejudice or condescension. In his letter to Philemon, Onesimus's owner, Paul wrote these words of encouragement and reconciliation: "Perhaps he [Onesimus] was for this reason separated from you for a while, that you would have him back forever, no longer as a slave, but more than a slave, a beloved brother, especially to me, but how much more to you, both in the flesh and in the Lord" (vv. 15–16). Through the power of the gospel, a former Pharisee now considered himself to be the brother of a Gentile runaway slave. He similarly instructed Philemon to receive Onesimus back with the love of one family member for another. Though Paul's background could not have been more different from that of Onesimus, those differences were no obstacle to fellowship and friendship, since every believer is a new creature in Christ (2 Cor. 5:16–17). For Paul, the slave of Christ, it was his joy to sacrificially serve any other member of his Master's house (cf. 1 Cor. 9:19).

The apostle James also confronted prejudice in his epistle—specifically on the part of the wealthy toward those who were poor. In chapter 2, he instructed his readers:

> My brethren, do not hold your faith in our glorious Lord Jesus Christ with an attitude of personal favoritism. For if a man comes into your assembly with a gold ring and dressed in fine clothes, and there also comes in a poor man in dirty clothes, and you pay special attention to the one who is wearing the fine clothes, and say, "You sit here in a good place," and you say to the poor man, "You stand over there, or sit down by my footstool," have you not made distinctions among yourselves, and become judges with evil motives? . . . If you show partiality, you are committing sin. (vv. 1–4, 9)

Such a warning is still needed in the church today. Prejudice and partiality have no place within the body of Christ. We were all unworthy slaves of sin, until Christ rescued us due to no merit of our own. We are all, now, the slaves of Christ, called to obey Him and to follow in His example of love and self-sacrifice. Consequently, we can serve one another in humility and gladness, no matter our ethnic or socioeconomic differences, knowing that we are all accountable to the same heavenly Master.

Slavery Magnifies Grace

A third paradox to consider is this: our slavery to Christ magnifies the wonder of His infinite grace. We have already discussed the fact that belonging to Christ as His slave is an infinite privilege (in chapter 6). But it is important to understand that our service to Him is also an undeserved gift—one we both receive and accomplish by His grace. Our ability to serve Him is only possible because He enables us to do so "by the strength which God supplies; so that in all things God may be glorified through Jesus Christ" (1 Peter 4:11).

God certainly does not need our acts of service (Acts 17:25; cf. Mark 10:45). Yet, He allows us the privilege of belonging to Him so that we might fully delight in Him, and in so doing, experience the true satisfaction and joy that come from knowing Him. Such is the essence of eternal life—as Jesus prayed in John 17:3, "This is eternal life, that they may know You, the only true God, and Jesus Christ whom You have sent." Eternal life is not merely a quantity of life, but a quality of life, one in which believers enjoy the inexhaustible and unsurpassed blessings that come from intimate fellowship with God, both in this life and the next.

In Matthew 6:24, Jesus told His hearers, "No one can serve two masters; for either he will hate the one and love the other, or he will be devoted to one and despise the other. You cannot serve God and wealth." Commenting on this verse, John Piper observed:

> How do we "serve money"? Not by helping money out or providing anything for money. But by calculating all our lives to benefit maximally from money. We govern all our decisions so as to maximize the delights of money. So with God. So behind Jesus' word about not serving money but serving God is the assumption that serving God means living so as to experience the fullness of God as our Treasure. . . . [T]he uniqueness of our Christian slavery is this: the Master is overwhelmingly all supplying so that even our servitude itself is a gift from his sovereign grace.[9]

Thus the apostle Paul could tell the Corinthians that, even in his sacrificial labors on Christ's behalf, all must be attributed to God's grace. "But by the grace of God I am what I am, and His grace toward me did not prove vain; but I labored even more than all of them, yet not I, but the grace of God with me" (1 Cor. 15:10). Similarly, all Christians are called to "work out [their] salvation with fear and trembling" while recognizing that "it is God who is at work in [them], both to will and to work for His good pleasure" (Phil. 2:12–13). The astonishing reality is that God not only calls us to be dutiful slaves; He also enables us to be faithful to that calling. Moreover, having empowered our service to Him, He then promises to eternally reward us for the faithfulness He has graciously enabled.

The slavery metaphor not only magnifies grace; it also showcases

---

9. John Piper, in an unpublished e-mail dated February 9, 2010. Used by permission.

love. As one author has explained, "Matching the paradox of 'slavery in freedom' is the paradox of 'love in slavery.' Within Christian freedom there is slavery; within Christian slavery there is love. This prevents freedom from becoming unbridled license and prevents slavery from becoming cringing bondage."[10] Slavery to Christ is much more than mere *duty*; it is motivated by a heart filled with loving *devotion* and pure *delight*. Because God first loved us and sent His Son to redeem us from sin, we now love Him—longing from the heart to worship, honor, and obey Him in everything. Our slavery to Him is not drudgery but a joy-filled privilege made possible by His saving grace and the Spirit's continued working in our lives. As loyal citizens and grateful children, we now serve our King and our Father out of hearts brimming with thankfulness. To be Christ's slave is a wonderful and blessed reality; to be His "*doulos* is not partially sweet and partially sour, but totally sweet."[11]

All of this underscores the magnanimous character of our loving Master. His bondage is true freedom. His yoke is easy and His burden is light. What He has required, He has also enabled by His grace. And He calls us to obey, not because He needs us but because He knows that we need Him. After all, it is only in relationship with Him that our souls can be satisfied. Only by delighting in Him can we experience true joy and eternal life. As Augustine famously prayed in his *Confessions*, "You awake us to delight in praising You, for You have made us for Yourself, and our hearts are restless until they find their rest in You."[12]

---

10. Murray J. Harris, *Slave of Christ* (Downers Grove, IL: InterVarsity Press, 1999), 155.

11. Ibid., 142.

12. Augustine, *Confessions*, 1, in Jay P. Green, trans., *Saint Augustine's Confessions* (LaVergne, TN: Lightning Source, 2001), 1.

Slavery Pictures Salvation

A fourth and final paradox is found in this glorious reality: God has expressed the riches of our salvation using the symbolism of slavery. This truth, of course, has been the theme of this entire book. In eternity past, God chose those whom He would save. In our own lifetime, He rescued us from slavery to sin and delivered us into the kingdom of His dear Son. Christ's atoning work on the cross redeemed us, such that we were purchased by Him; and having been bought with a price, we are now His possession. We have been liberated from sin, and now as slaves to righteousness, we possess a glorious freedom that will be ours for all of eternity.

But the language of slavery does more than merely picture the gospel. In fact, it is central to the message of salvation. That is because the slavery metaphor points to the reality of Christ's lordship, and the lordship of Christ is essential to the biblical gospel.

The gospel message is not simply a *plan* of salvation; it is a call to embrace the *Person* of salvation. And He is both Savior *and* Lord; the two cannot be separated. To truly come to Christ is to willingly surrender your heart, mind, and will—the whole person—to the Master. Mere lip service to Jesus' lordship is nothing more than hypocrisy (Titus 1:16)—a false profession that cannot save (Matt. 7:23; Luke 6:46). Likewise, to preach Christ as Savior but not as Lord is to present a gospel message that is incomplete. In the words of missionary-martyr Jim Elliot:

> [It is a] twentieth-century heresy that Christ is Savior only by right, Lord by "option" of the "believer." This denial of the only Master and Lord, preach[es] only half of His person, declaring only partially the truth as it is in Jesus Christ[.] [The gospel] must be preached with

the full apprehension of who He is, the demanding Lord as well as the delivering Savior. . . . Denial of the lordship of the Lord. *That* is disobedience which in any way makes pliable the requirement of God, for it makes God not God.[13]

The gospel, proclaimed in its fullness, necessarily includes the lordship of Jesus Christ. As Paul would tell the Romans, "*If you confess with your mouth Jesus as Lord,* and believe in your heart that God raised Him from the dead, you will be saved" (Rom. 10:9, emphasis added). When asked, "What must I do to be saved?" he similarly instructed the Philippian jailer, "Believe in the *Lord* Jesus, and you will be saved" (Acts 16:31, emphasis added). In explaining the gospel to the Jews on the day of Pentecost, Peter ended his sermon with these words: "Therefore let all the house of Israel know for certain that God has made Him both *Lord and Christ*—this Jesus whom you crucified" (Acts 2:36, emphasis added).

Along those lines, the New Testament consistently places an emphasis on repentance in its evangelistic calls to the lost. Jesus Himself preached, "*Repent* and believe in the gospel" (Mark 1:15, emphasis added; cf. Luke 24:47). At Pentecost, Peter proclaimed, "*Repent,* and each of you be baptized in the name of Jesus Christ for the forgiveness of your sins; and you will receive the gift of the Holy Spirit" (Acts 2:38, emphasis added; cf. Acts 5:31). Paul told the philosophers on Mars Hill, "God is now declaring to men that all people everywhere should *repent*" (Acts 17:30, emphasis added; cf. 20:21). Emphasizing the obedient nature of saving faith, John wrote,

---

13. Jim Elliot, in Elisabeth Elliot, ed., *The Journals of Jim Elliot* (Old Tappan, NJ: Revell, 1978), 253. The date for this journal entry is June 7, 1950.

"He who does not *obey* the Son will not see life, but the wrath of God abides on him" (John 3:36, emphasis added). The writer to the Hebrews similarly said that Christ "became to all those who *obey* Him the source of eternal salvation" (Heb. 5:9, emphasis added). Though such language contradicts the "easy-believism" of some contemporary evangelists, it accords perfectly with the paradigm of first-century slavery.

To be clear, salvation is by faith alone. Yet genuine saving faith is never alone. It inevitably produces "fruit in keeping with repentance" (Matt. 3:8), thereby evidencing a transformed heart. The one who claims to know Christ yet continues in patterns of unrepentant sin betrays the credibility of his profession of faith (1 John 1:6). By the same token, the one who claims to belong to Christ yet remains wholly enslaved to sin, deceives himself as to his spiritual condition. True slaves of Christ have been liberated from sin and freed to righteousness. Their lives bear witness to that reality. Having been saved by grace, they were "created in Christ Jesus for good works" (Eph. 2:10). Now they walk in joyful obedience, motivated out of their heartfelt love for the Master (John 14:15). As Charles Spurgeon explained:

> Every true Christian pronounces this phrase, "Jesus our Lord," with the emphasis of *unreservedness*. We desire that Christ Jesus should be our Lord in everything and Lord over every part of our being. . . . He who truly loves Jesus, and who knows that he is one of those who are redeemed by him, says with all his heart that Jesus is Lord, his absolute Sovereign, his Despot, if that word be used in the sense of Christ having unlimited monarchy and supreme sway over the soul. Yea, O "Jesus our Lord," thou shalt be

the autocratic, imperial Master of our heart, and of the whole dominion of our manhood![14]

Thus we end this book where we began—asking the question,
what does it mean to be a Christian? Whether we examine the national
identity of Israel after the exodus from Egypt, or the self-identification
of the apostolic writers, or the nomenclature used by early Christian
martyrs—we find ourselves continually confronted with a concept as
foreign to our Western minds as it is radical and profound. Yet if we
are to fully appreciate what it means to follow Christ, we must embrace
the life-changing implications of this vital concept.

To be a Christian is to be a slave of Christ.

---

14. Charles Spurgeon, "Jesus Our Lord," *Metropolitan Tabernacle Pulpit* (Pasadena, TX: Pilgrim
Publications, 1977), 48:558. Italics original.

Appendix

Voices from
Church History

The Shepherd of Hermas (c. 130)

The Shepherd of Hermas *is one of the oldest Christian documents outside of the New Testament. It refers to believers as "slaves of God" on a number of occasions, as evidenced from the excerpt below.*[1] *Other ancient Christian documents evidence a similar understanding of the Christian life. For example, the* First Epistle of Clement of Rome *(written around AD 95), refers to God as "the Master" in some twenty passages.*[2] *Similarly, in his letter to the Philadelphians, Ignatius (c. 50–c. 110) wrote about the "bishop together with the presbytery and the deacons, my fellow slaves."*[3]

In recounting a vision Hermas had reportedly received, he wrote:

I replied, "What sorts of evil things, Lord, must we refrain from doing?" "Listen," he said: "from adultery and sexual immorality, from lawless drunkenness, from evil luxury, from an abundance of foods, extravagant wealth, boasting, pride, and haughtiness, from lying, slander, and hypocrisy, from bearing a grudge and speaking any blasphemy. These are the most wicked of all the deeds of human life. And so, *the slave of God must refrain from doing them.* For the one who does not refrain from these cannot live to God. Hear now as well about the

---

1. According to James S. Jeffers, "Hermas identifies himself and other Christians as the slaves of God (*Vis.* 1.2.4; 4.1.3; *Mand.* 3.4; *Sim.* 8.6.5). The implication of these passages is that Christians owe God the same obedience that masters require of their slaves" ("Jewish and Christian Families in First-Century Rome," in Karl P. Donfried and Peter Richardson, eds., *Judaism and Christianity in First-Century Rome* [Grand Rapids: Eerdmans, 1998], 148).

2. James Aloysius Kleist notes this about Clement's first *Epistle to the Corinthians.* "In about 20 passages in this epistle Clement speaks of God as 'the Master,' a designation not common in modern speech. The idea is the same that prompted St. Paul to call himself the *doulos* or 'slave' of Christ" (*The Epistles of St. Clement of Rome and St. Ignatius of Antioch* [Mahwah, NJ: Paulist Press, 1946], 106–7n35).

3. Ignatius, *Letter to the Philadelphians*, 4, in Bart D. Ehrman, trans., *The Apostolic Fathers* (Cambridge, Mass.: Harvard University, 2003), I:287.

things that follow these." "Are there yet other wicked deeds, Lord?" I asked. "Yes indeed," he said, "*there are many from which the slave of God must refrain*: robbery, lying, fraud, bearing false witness, greed, evil desire, deception, vanity, arrogance, and as many things as are similar to these. Do these things not seem wicked to you?" "Yes indeed," I said, "very wicked for the slaves of God." "And so *it is necessary for the one enslaved to God to refrain from these things.*"[4]

Polycarp (c. 69–c. 155)

In his Letter to the Philippians, *Polycarp wrote,*

For you know that you have been saved by a gracious gift—not from works but by the will of God through Jesus Christ. Therefore, *bind up your loose robes and serve as God's slaves in reverential fear and truth,* abandoning futile reasoning and the error that deceives many, and believing in the one who raised our Lord Jesus Christ from the dead and gave him glory and a throne at his right hand. *Everything in heaven and on earth is subject to him; everything that breathes will serve him;* he is coming as a judge of the living and the dead; and God will hold those who disobey him accountable for his blood.[5]

Second-Century Martyrs

In a letter from the Churches of Lyons and Vienne to the Church of Asia:

---

4. *Shepherd of Hermas*, Exposition on the Eighth Commandment, 38.3–6, in Ehrman, *The Apostolic Fathers* (Cambridge, Mass.: Harvard, 2005), II:269–71.

5. Polycarp, *Letter to the Philippians*, 1–2, in Ehrman, *The Apostolic Fathers* (2003), I:335.

The dwellers in Vienne and Lyons of Gaul, *slaves of Christ*, to the brethren in Asia and Phrygia who have the same faith and hope of redemption with us, peace and grace and glory from God the Father and our Lord Christ Jesus. The greatness of this our tribulation, the furious rage of the Gentiles against the saints, and what things the blessed martyrs have suffered, we are not able exactly to express by word, or comprehend in writing.[6]

Ambrosiaster (c. 366–c. 384)

He [the apostle Paul] says this because through the law of faith he has died to the law of Moses. *For the one who is liberated from it "dies" and lives to God, becoming his slave, purchased by Christ.*[7]

John Chrysostom (c. 347–407)

[I]n the things that relate to Christ, both [slaves and masters] are equal: and *just as you are the slave of Christ, so also is your master. . . .* [I]t is possible for one who is a slave not to be a slave; and for one who is a freeman to be a slave. "And how can one be a slave and not a slave?" When he does all for God: when he feigns nothing, and does nothing out of eye-service towards men: that is how one who is a slave to men can be free. Or again, how does one who is free become a slave [of sin]? When he serves men in any evil service, either for gluttony or

---

6. Eusebius, *Ecclesiastical History*, 5.1–4, in John Allen Giles, trans., *The Writings of the Early Christians of the Second Century* (London: John Russell Smith, 1857), 222.

7. *Corpus Scriptorum Ecclesiasticorum Latinorum*, 81.3:28.21–3, in Eric Plumer's critical notes in *Augustine's Commentary on Galatians* (New York: Oxford University Press, 2003), 30n153.

desire of wealth or for office's sake. For such a one, though he be free, is more of a slave than any man. . . .

Such a thing is Christianity; in slavery it bestows freedom. . . . [After all,] the real slavery is that of sin. And if you are not a slave in this sense, be bold and rejoice. No one shall have power to do you any wrong, having the temperament which cannot be enslaved. But if you are a slave to sin, even though you be ten thousand times free you have no good of your freedom.[8]

First there is the freeing from sin, and then there is the making of slaves of righteousness, which is better than any freedom. For God has done the same as if a person were to take an orphan who had been carried away by savages into their own country, and was not only to free him from captivity but to set a kind of father over him and raise him to a very great dignity. This is what has happened in our case. For it was not just that God freed us from our old evils; He also led us into the life of angels. He opened the way for us to enjoy the best life, handing us over to the safekeeping of righteousness and killing our former evils, putting the old man in us to death and bringing us to eternal life.[9]

Augustine (354–430)

Writing about Augustine, Gerald Bonner noted that "personal experience, as reported in the Confessions, *had persuaded him that in the last*

---

8. Chrysostom, *Homilies on First Corinthians*, Homily 19.5–6 (on 1 Cor. 7:22–23), quoted in Philip Schaff, *A Select Library of the Nicene and Post-Nicene Fathers of the Christian Church* (New York: Christian Literature Company, 1889), XII.108–9. English translation updated for readability.

9. John Chrysostom, *Homilies on Romans*, 11, quoted in Gerald Bray, ed., *Romans, Ancient Christian Commentary on Scripture* (Downers Grove, IL: InterVarsity, 1998), 170.

resort human freedom could only be relative: only by becoming enslaved to God could one escape being a slave to sin.[10] *Following are several places where Augustine's emphasis on that concept can be seen.*

Does your Lord not deserve to have you as his trustworthy slave?[11]

If then he, one with the Father, equal to the Father, God from God, God with God, co-eternal, immortal, equally unchanging, equally timeless, equally creator and disposer of times, if he because he came in time, *took the form of a slave, and was found in appearance as a man* (Phil 2:7), then he seeks his Father's glory, not his own. What should you, O man, do, you who seek your own glory whenever you do anything good, while when you do something bad, you figure out ways to blame God?

Take a look at yourself; you are a creature, acknowledge the creator; *you are a slave, do not disdain the master*; you have been adopted, but not on your merits. Seek the glory of the one from whom you have received this grace, O adopted child, seek the glory of the one whose glory was sought by his only true born Son.[12]

Charles Hodge (1797–1878)

All Christians . . . were bought with a price. That is, purchased by Christ with his most precious blood, 1 Pet. 1, 18.19. Ye belong to

---

10. Gerald Bonner, "Anti-Pelagian Works," in Allan Fitzgerald, ed., *Augustine through the Ages: An Encyclopedia* (Grand Rapids: Eerdmans, 1999), 43.

11. Augustine, "Sermon 159," in John E. Rottelle, trans., *Sermons* (Hyde Park, NY: New City Press, 1992), 124.

12. Augustine, *Homilies on the Gospel of John 1–40*, Homily 29. Translated by Edmund Hill (Hyde Park, NY: New City Press, 2009), 495.

him; ye are his slaves, and should therefore act accordingly; and not be the slaves of men. The slave of one master cannot be the slave of another. One who is redeemed by Christ, who feels that he belongs to him, that his will is the supreme rule of action, and who performs all his duties, not as a man-pleaser, but as doing service as to the Lord, and not to men, Eph. 6, 6. 7, is inwardly free, whatever his external relations may be. . . . They [the Corinthian believers] all belonged to Christ. To him their allegiance was due. They, therefore, whether bond or free, should act in obedience to him, and not in obedience to men.[13]

Charles Spurgeon (1834–1892)

Make no reserve, exercise no choice but obey his command. When you know what he commands, do not hesitate, question, or try to avoid it, but "do it": do it at once, do it heartily, do it cheerfully, do it to the full. It is but a little thing that, as our Lord has bought us with the price of his own blood, we should be his servants. The apostles frequently call themselves the bond-slaves of Christ. *Where our Authorized Version softly puts it "servant" it really is "bond-slave." The early saints delighted to count themselves Christ's absolute property, bought by him, owned by him, and wholly at his disposal.* Paul even went so far as to rejoice that he had the marks of his Master's brand on him, and he cries, "Let no man trouble me: for I bear in my body the marks of the Lord Jesus." There was the end of all debate: he was the Lord's, and the marks of

---

13. Charles Hodge, *Exposition of the First Epistle to the Corinthians* (New York: Robert Carter & Brothers, 1878), 125.

the scourges, the rods, and the stones were the broad-arrow of the King which marked Paul's body as the property of Jesus the Lord. Now if the saints of old time gloried in obeying Christ, I pray that you and I, forgetting the sect to which we may belong, or even the nation of which we form a part, may feel that our first object in life is to obey our Lord and not to follow a human leader, or to promote a religious or political party. This one thing we mean to do, and so follow the advice of Solomon as he says, "Let thine eyes look right on, and let thine eyelids look straight before thee." Beloved, let us endeavor to be obedient in the minute as well as in the greater matters, for it is in details that true obedience is best seen.[14]

We are to wait upon our Master humbly, reverently, feeling it an honour to do anything for him. We are to be self-surrendered, given up henceforth to the Lord, free men, and yet most truly serfs of this Great Emperor. We are never so free as when we own our sacred serfdom. . . . *Often Paul calls himself the servant of the Lord, and even the slave of Christ, and he glories in the branding iron's marks upon his flesh.* "I bear," says he, "in my body the marks of the Lord Jesus; henceforth let no man trouble me." *We count it liberty to bear the bonds of Christ.* We reckon this to be supremest freedom for we sing with the psalmist, "I am thy servant; I am thy servant. Thou hast loosed my bonds." "Bind the sacrifice with cords, even with cords to the horns of the altar." Such is the conduct which our servitude to our Lord requires.[15]

14. Charles Spurgeon, "Eyes Right," *Metropolitan Tabernacle Pulpit* (Pasadena, TX: Pilgrim Publications, 1974), 34:689.

15. Charles Spurgeon, "The Way to Honor," sermon no. 1118, in *Metropolitan Tabernacle Pulpit* (Pasadena, TX: Pilgrim Publications, 1981), 19:356–57.

Every true Christian pronounces this phrase, "Jesus our Lord," with the emphasis of *unreservedness.* We desire that Christ Jesus should be our Lord in everything and Lord over every part of our being. . . . He who truly loves Jesus, and who knows that he is one of those who are redeemed by him, says with all his heart that Jesus is Lord, his absolute Sovereign, his Despot, if that word be used in the sense of Christ having unlimited monarchy and supreme sway over the soul. Yea, O "Jesus our Lord," thou shalt be the autocratic, imperial Master of our heart, and of the whole dominion of our manhood![16]

Alexander Maclaren (1826–1910)

The true position, then, for a man is to be God's slave. The harsh, repellent features of that wicked institution assume an altogether different character when they become the features of my relation to Him. Absolute submission, unconditional obedience, on the slave's part; and on the part of the Master complete ownership, the right of life and death, the right of disposing of all goods and chattels, the right of separating husband and wife, parents and children, the right of issuing commandments without a reason, the right to expect that those commandments shall be swiftly, unhesitatingly, punctiliously, and completely performed—these things inhere in our relation to God. Blessed the man who has learned that they do, and has accepted them as his highest glory and the security of his most blessed life! For, brethren, *such submission, absolute and unconditional, the blending and the absorption of my own will in His will, is the secret of all that makes manhood glorious and great and happy.*

---

16. Charles Spurgeon, "Jesus Our Lord," *Metropolitan Tabernacle Pulpit* (Pasadena, TX: Pilgrim Publications, 1977), 48:558. Italics original.

Remember, however, that in the New Testament these names of slave and owner are transferred to Christians and Jesus Christ. "The Servant" has His slaves; and He who is God's Servant, and does not His own will but the Father's will, has us for His servants, imposes His will upon us, and we are bound to render to Him a revenue of entire obedience like that which He hath laid at His Father's feet.

Such slavery is the only freedom. Liberty does not mean doing as you like, it means liking as you ought, and doing that. He only is free who submits to God in Christ, and thereby overcomes himself and the world and all antagonism, and is able to do that which it is his life to do. A prison out of which we do not desire to go is no restraint, and the will which coincides with law is the only will that is truly free. You talk about the bondage of obedience. Ah! "the weight of too much liberty" is a far sorer bondage. They are the slaves who say, "Let us break His bonds asunder, and cast away His cords from us"; and they are the free men who say, "Lord, put Thy blessed shackles on my arms, and impose Thy will upon my will, and fill my heart with Thy love; and then will and hands will move freely and delightedly." "If the Son make you free, ye shall be free indeed."

Such slavery is the only nobility. In the wicked old empires, as in some of their modern survivals today, viziers and prime ministers were mostly drawn from the servile classes. It is so in God's kingdom. They who make themselves God's slaves are by Him made kings and priests, and shall reign with Him on earth. If we are slaves, then are we sons and heirs of God through Jesus Christ. . . .

The Servant-Son makes us slaves and sons. It matters nothing to me that Jesus Christ perfectly fulfilled the law of God; it is so much the better for Him, but of no value for me, unless He has the power of making me like Himself. And He has it, and if you will trust yourselves to Him, and give your hearts to Him, and ask Him to govern you, He will govern you; and if you will abandon your false liberty which is servitude, and take the sober freedom which is obedience, then He will bring you to share in His temper of joyful service; and even we may be able to say, "My meat and my drink is to do the will of Him that sent me," and truly saying that, we shall have the key to all delights.[17]

R. C. H. Lenski (1864–1936)

[We are to be] presenting ourselves and our members as δουλοι ["slaves"] to God after we have been freed from the dominion of sin and are happy and blessed slaves of God. Here we have Luther's "live under him in his kingdom and serve him," etc. The participle [in Romans 14:18] means, "being a slave and working as a slave." The implication is not as it is in διακονειν ["to serve"], rendering service for Christ, doing as much as we can for him; but in all that we do having no will of our own, being directed and controlled only by Christ's will, he being our Κύριος, our only Lord and Master. . . . *He who, as a slave to Christ, submits his will to him in all he does "is well-pleasing to God" and need never fear to stand before his judgment seat.*[18]

J. Campbell White (1870–1962)

Speaking at the 1906 international conference of the Student Volunteer Movement for Foreign Missions, J. Campbell White challenged his audience with these words:

---

17. Alexander Maclaren, *Expositions of Holy Scripture, the Acts* (n.p.: Bibliolife, 2007), 148–49.

18. R. C. H. Lenski, *Interpretation of Saint Paul's Epistle* (Minneapolis: Augsburg Fortress, 2008), 843.

Is it true, or is it false, that *Jesus Christ is the only rightful owner and Lord of our lives?* Martin Luther thought it was true when he said, "If anyone would knock on the door of my breast and say, 'Who lives here?' I would not reply, 'Martin Luther,' but would say, 'The Lord Jesus Christ.'" Paul gave expression to the greatest practical reality of his life when he said, "I am crucified with Christ; nevertheless, I live; yet not I, but Christ liveth in me." "For to me to live is Christ." And he not only regarded himself as the slave of Christ, but he regarded that attitude as the normal and rightful one of every disciple of Christ. "Ye are not your own; for ye are bought with a price; therefore, glorify God in your body, and in your spirit." "Ye are Christ's; and Christ is God's." "Feed the Church of God, which he hath purchased with his own blood." "I beseech you, therefore, brethren, by the mercies of God, that ye present your bodies a living sacrifice, holy, acceptable unto God, which is your reasonable service." And our Lord Himself regarded this as the only right attitude of every follower of His toward Himself. "Ye call me Master and Lord; and ye say well; for so I am."

This lordship and ownership of Jesus Christ applies not only to our lives, but it carries with it all our possessions and powers. . . . There can be no possible question that Jesus Christ regards Himself as the owner and Lord of our life. For us the practical question is, Have we recognized His ownership and His lordship, and are we living in that attitude toward Him.

. . . I ask myself, as I ask you tonight, whether there is anything so divine that we can do with this life of ours as to bind it in perpetual voluntary slavery to Jesus Christ for lost humanity's sake, and to say to Him: "If God will show me anything that I can do for the redemption of this world that I have not yet attempted, by His grace I will undertake it at once; for I cannot, I dare not go up to judgment until I have done the utmost that God expects me to do to diffuse His glory throughout the whole world."[19]

Jim Elliot (1927–1956)

Jim Elliot was one of five American missionaries to Ecuador who were martyred by the Waodani Indians. He is famous for his statement "He is no fool who gives what he cannot keep to gain that which he cannot lose."[20] In another journal entry, commenting on the opening verses of Jude, he wrote:

Certain men in the group to whom Jude wrote had turned the grace of God into loose living, denying the only Master and Lord, Jesus Christ. This was written for my day: For today I hear of men preaching that grace means freedom to live unrestrained lives apart from any standard of moral purity, declaring "we are not under law, we are under grace." Grace turned into ἀσέλγεια ["licentiousness"]! Combined with this is the twentieth-century heresy that Christ is Savior only by right, Lord by "option" of the "believer." This denial of the only Master and Lord, preach[es] only half of His person, declaring only partially the truth as it is in Jesus Christ[.] [The gospel] must be preached with the full apprehension of who He is, the demanding Lord as well as the delivering Savior. . . . Denial of the lordship of the Lord. That is disobedience which in any way makes pliable the requirement of God, for it makes God not God.[21]

---

19. J. Campbell White, "The Ownership and Lordship of Jesus Christ," in *Students and the Modern Missionary Crusade* (New York: Student Volunteer Movement for Foreign Missions, 1906), 29, 36.

20. Jim Elliot, in Elisabeth Elliott, ed., *The Journals of Jim Elliot* (Old Tappan, NJ: Revell, 1978), 174, journal entry dated October 28, 1949.

21. Ibid., 253, journal entry dated June 7, 1950.

About the Author

Widely known for his thorough, candid approach to teaching God's Word, John MacArthur is a popular author and conference speaker and has served as pastor-teacher of Grace Community Church in Sun Valley, California, since 1969. John and his wife, Patricia, have four grown children and fifteen grandchildren.

John's pulpit ministry has been extended around the globe through his media ministry, Grace to You, and its satellite offices in seven countries. In addition to producing daily radio programs for nearly two thousand English and Spanish radio outlets worldwide, Grace to You distributes books, software, audiotapes, and CDs by John MacArthur.

John is president of The Master's College and Seminary and has written hundreds of books and study guides, each one biblical and practical. Best-selling titles include *The Gospel According to Jesus, Truth War, The Murder of Jesus, Twelve Ordinary Men, Twelve Extraordinary Women*, and *The MacArthur Study Bible*, a 1998 ECPA Gold Medallion recipient.

To help you dig deeper into what it means to be Christ's slave,
Dr. MacArthur has prepared a helpful guide for your personal
or group study. Includes probing questions, recommended
additional reading, and extended Bible passages.

ISBN: 978-1-4002-0291-1